PRAISE FOR

These essays are a treat to savor. Their quality lies not in prescribing a route to prosperity, but rather in gently prompting us to set our compass to a path that leads to fairness and value for all.

> —**Dr. Juan Rivera**, Cardiologist, Chief Medical
> Correspondent Univision

"*Fair Value* is a must-read for business leaders who desire to improve corporate culture in order to more fully engage all stakeholders in maximizing value for all. Mr. Opdeweegh's writings are a rare and honest look into the thinking and values of one of the preeminent global business leaders of our time."

> —**Mark J. Gendregske**, Principal, St. Charles Holdings

"Rarely do you see such a close coupling of an author's reflections and how they live their lives—this is Jos! Reflective, philosophical, questioning, translating to practical implementation and refreshingly focused on all aspects of society as beneficiaries of vision and leadership."

> —**Gary Kennedy**, Board Chairman, Greencore Group PLC

"A different kind of management book. A soulful series of reflections on values and virtues in business, which manages to be at once both profoundly personal and yet universal."

> —**Jonathan Obermeister**, Managing Partner, Change Agency

"*Fair Value* poignantly points to the key issue in many businesses today—how to win the mindshare and trust of employees, customers, and suppliers by treating them each fairly and with integrity."

> —**Tim Oglesby**, Chief Technology and Transformation
> Officer, Santo Remedio LLC

Fair Value: Reflections on Good Business

by Jozef J Opdeweegh

ISBN 978-1-64663-457-6

Illustrations by JB Hopkins

Published by

◤ köehlerbooks™

3705 Shore Drive
Virginia Beach, VA 23455
800-435-4811
www.koehlerbooks.com

FAIR
VALUE

reflections on good business

JOZEF J OPDEWEEGH

VIRGINIA BEACH
CAPE CHARLES

CONTENTS

WHEN GEESE FLY AS ONE, THEY TAKE
TURNS TO LEAD, TO FALL BACK
AND SHELTER — INSTINCTIVE, ELEGANT GRACE.

This book is dedicated to all those who live by values of respect, decency, and care for others.

History shows that the making of a better world is not straight forward—that while progress thrives on a respect for science and analysis, we must pay equal attention to our feelings and desires.

Throughout my career, I've been inspired by those who are able to put the collective good above individual gain, who are liberal and open-minded, who value intellect and analysis . . . but who also understand that some of our deepest concerns are not reducible to logic.

These are the tenacious seekers of progress—making contributions, big and small, neat and messy, to the collective endeavor we call life. The essays in this book are a homage to them and all they have taught me.

Jozef J Opdeweegh

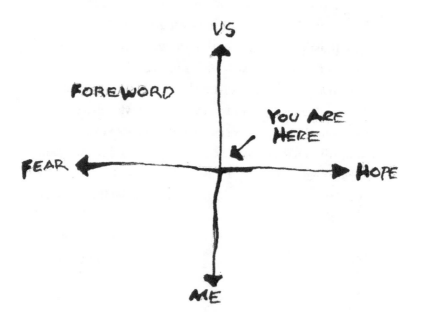

OUR ~~CHOICES ARE DETERMINED BY THE PATHS WE TAKE.~~

OUR PATHS ARE DETERMINED BY THE CHOICES WE MAKE.

FOREWORD

VS

YOU ARE HERE

FEAR ← → HOPE

ME

FOREWORD

ON ARRIVING AS CEO at the electronics distribution company where I was Chairman, Jozef Opdeweegh encountered some significant challenges. Within two weeks, we received an offer to acquire the business, and after a bid battle with competing offers, eventually agreed a sale to a much larger US competitor.

During this period of both business and personal uncertainty, including the relocation of his family from the US to London, Jozef provided outstanding leadership, gaining the respect, and also the affection, of stakeholders and colleagues alike. Having been a CEO myself, and having served on many boards with capable CEOs over the years, Jozef is to be compared with the most talented—his grasp of the financials, his speed at getting to the nub of an issue, his authority, swift decision-making and indeed, his courage are all exceptional qualities. Jozef was a tough but fair taskmaster too, working all hours himself but with an empathy and good humor which endeared him to his colleagues. At his farewell party, following the sale of the company, they presented him with an English gentleman's shooting outfit of tweed plus-fours, with which he was highly delighted, donning it immediately!

As a global business person, having worked in a variety of roles in Belgium, Canada, the USA and the UK, Jozef brings a breadth of experience to the concepts of fairness and trust. But above all, he brings to the debate—and to his writing—an openness and authenticity, which anyone who's worked with him would recognize.

In reading *Fair Value*, I've rediscovered that refreshing approach, one which is highly thought-provoking, but which doesn't propose prescriptive theories—something of a rarity in my experience.

The essays themselves are founded on the belief that core values should underpin our approach and decisions as leaders—and that our *living* and *creating* value are intrinsically linked. They also demonstrate an evolving mind-set, recognizing that our beliefs and values can change over time, rather than being fixed. The practical insights which Jozef offers strike a chord with me as they will with others, grounded as they are in his rich and varied experience.

While reading *Fair Value*, it reminded me that although many leaders can talk at length about values, they often sound glib or superficial, their words seldom straying from the *corporate speak* which by its very ubiquity often stifles debate.

Jozef, however, speaks from the heart. I recommend his reflections to all who wish to consider the world's challenges more deeply – there is a lot to learn here.

Val Gooding, CBE

INTRODUCTION

HOW DO WE BEST create shareholder value?

Such was the question at the forefront of my mind when my career began. I'd been taught the pursuit was essential; that the purpose of a business was to fulfil its mission while delivering returns in excess of costs, providing a sustainable flow of profit and cash. The quest would not be easy, but it was more strategic than philosophical and I threw myself into the task.

Thirty years on, I'm glad I did. For in starting out, and in business in general, there's a hands-on experiential element that no classroom MBA can teach. There's also an essential truth in the axiom above: the competitive pursuit of profit remains the driving force of companies across the globe, and rightly so, for without sustainable returns our efforts will ultimately fail.

But if the pursuit of profit remains necessary, it is no longer sufficient. Over the course of my career, our understanding of the role and purpose of business has shifted. And with that comes a subtle but vital adjustment to the way we pose and hear the opening question. As a young man, my mind was principally attuned to the words *create* and *value*; today it is *how* and *best* which ring just as loudly in my ears.

And it is the echoes of these subtleties, their harmony and counter points, which are the chief concerns and genesis of this book. The answers are not straightforward, or as logically resolvable as we might wish them to be. Indeed, the questions which prompt them are posed in a context of a world that's not only changing, but doing so at an ever-faster pace.

The pretext of these essays is that, on ground which is constantly moving, it is our core values—intangible though they may be—that are the constellation from which to plot our course. That doesn't make things easy—for all navigation involves modifying our plans, assessing what's ahead, making judgements on the paths to take. And often—like Polaris in the northern sky—the guiding light is not as bright or as clear as we would wish.

All of which is a means of saying that the thoughts which follow are not offered as a definitive guide to leadership. Rather, they are prompts to reflection, a sharing of what I've found, and no doubt a spark of challenge for those who disagree (which is a good thing when constructive and kindled with care). In essence, these writings are no more than my truth as I saw it at the time, with all the imperfections that come from this caveat.

It would, however, be disingenuous not to affirm that the essays are also—at least in part—a response to the politics and events of recent years. The rise of populism, the question of Brexit, and the emergence of a new global economic order have all, to some extent, influenced the matters that concern me. It would be insincere too, not to declare that at times the contextual landscape has seemed dark. As I write this introduction, we are in the midst of a global pandemic that poses perhaps some of the greatest challenges for leadership—and values— that we have faced in decades.

Many of the pieces that follow have been published elsewhere. While it was tempting to update them to take account of developments, I believe to have done so would be untrue to their spirit. It would also falsely suggest I have greater foresight than anyone can possess. My preference is to beg forgiveness for those errors of perspective which inevitably arise when commenting at close quarters. As the saying goes, we can all see clearly in hindsight.

All journeys of worth will change us in their making. From Homer's *Odyssey* to Steinbeck's *The Grapes of Wrath*, we have three thousand years of literature attesting to this fact. And so, it's no surprise that, in crafting these essays, I too have changed—not in my beliefs, but in the way that reflection and experience enriches our understanding of what we hold most dear. That voyage is ongoing, and I hope it never ends.

I'm hopeful too for brighter times ahead. Values have never been more center stage. Leaders are more aware than ever of the need to act for the environment. Our commitments to diversity, rights, and freedoms will ultimately triumph over the politics of division and retrenchment. We can learn too—both as organizations and wider societies—from what, for progressive liberals such as myself, have at times felt like difficult years. Nobody has a monopoly on truth, and the concerns of those who feel left behind by progress are as legitimate as those who want to press ahead.

But enough context for now, the essays should hereafter speak for themselves.

They would not have been possible, however, without the support and wisdom of my colleagues, and mentors. I'm grateful for the trust they have shown, for all they have taught me and the lessons we have learned together. This book is tribute to that joint endeavor; my gratitude is heartfelt and humble.

Last but not least I must thank my family, whose care sustains me above all else. The passage of love through the generations is the greatest gift we can both give and receive. And yet always it is free. As the most vital of our values, it cannot be measured by any formula for returns. Rather, it is an end in itself, unbounded and infinite.

Jozef J Opdeweegh

FINDING OUR WAY IS LIKE
CHOOSING A KEY
—NOTES THAT WORK
TOGETHER + IN TENSION.

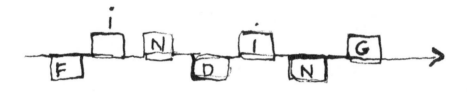

Let the watchwords of all our people be the old familiar watchwords of honesty, decency, fair-dealing, and commonsense . . . The welfare of each of us is dependent fundamentally upon the welfare of all of us.

Theodore Roosevelt

WHY I WRITE

SOME YEARS AGO, I sat with a friend, talking of the paths our careers had followed. The arc of the conversation was not so much our circumstances as those of our children, the journey in life they would take and how, as parents, we might guide them. And I recall him saying, "The one thing we can be sure of, is that whatever they do, it won't be as we imagine." I've thought often about that remark; it was one of those throw-away lines that I doubt he'd even remember and yet within it lies a truth that's relevant to us all.

Throughout my career, I've been privileged to work with many talented and wonderful people. My own journey is an indirect consequence of what they taught me, as well as what I experienced and observed along the way. Sure, there's been lots of hard work and ambition too—success of any substance is seldom about luck or who you know. But it's hubris for anyone in a senior role of a modern organization to believe in the myth of the *self-made man*—we are, all of us, interconnected and interdependent in navigating our way through life.

That idea of navigation—of the need for bearings and compass points—is something that earlier generations would have puzzled over. In researching our family histories, the vast majority of us will discover a depressing regularity of agricultural laborers or manual trades, with birth, marriage, and death recorded in the same or nearby parishes. Much that we might wish for more color in our ancestries, the reality is that the options and opportunities we have today are a relatively modern phenomenon.

There are, of course, exceptions: the emigration of pioneers to the new worlds, the consequences of slavery and conflicts, the mass movements of people in response to the Industrial Revolution. These are the seismic shifts that have shaped our societies and they remain relevant not only in the wakes they leave behind but in how they point to the possibility of events that elude our foresight. Commentators often cite the digital revolution as a contemporary example, but the rise of China from a Maoist backwater to a world-leading economy has had an equally significant impact on commerce and communities across the globe. The point is that change is all around us.

So, what does this have to do with my theme?

The answer goes back to that conversation with my friend. Central to why I write is the belief that, despite some claims to the contrary, the skills and experience of today have a relevance to the way we manage for the future. The particularities of circumstance are always different, but at the risk of stretching my metaphor, just as when walking in the mountains a knowledge of map and compass is essential, so too are the convictional equivalents in the careers and life paths we seek to choose. It's for this reason that my primary interest lies in the values and attitudes which underpin the ways we live and work together.

There's no shortage of popular books on personal growth or organizational best practice, and to be fair, there's much wisdom—as well as considerable bunkum—to be found there. The writings of contemporary thinkers such as Simon Sinek and Daniel Kahneman are part of a long and flexible tradition that stretches back through the likes of Tom Peters and Dale Carnegie (whose *How to Win*

Friends and Influence People is still in print and popular today) to the philosophies of Adam Smith and John Stuart Mill.

My own writings are less structured. It's never been my intent to offer a unified theory, or to spin the lessons I've learned—no doubt ever more thinly—into a pretense of something greater than they are. Rather, I simply want to share the practical insights that have most shaped my beliefs, and which, over thirty years of leadership practice, have proved the most resilient to changing times.

And isn't that actually how we live our lives? Save for religious beliefs, I doubt there's a leader out there who's guided every day by a single text or theory they once read. Rather, we collate and order our experiences, keeping some more front-of-mind than others and drawing on them as time or situation demands. These are the bearings and compass points I was referring to earlier. And in a sense, that's what I hope to lay down: an orientation, if you like, for the challenges and complications of leading a progressive organization—the seeking of improvement by degrees, in trial and often error, but always keeping faith with values that are grounded in truth and humanity.

I should add that the process of writing has in itself a uniquely helpful quality—for it requires us to choose. The act of putting pen to paper means we must decide what's important, how to order the issues and fit them together in a cohesive and logical manner. In that regard, it's the best tool I know to bring clarity to the conflicts and inconsistencies of our minds. In truth, words are not always up to the task, but at least in trying, we're able to glimpse something clearer than the clouded narratives we otherwise construct for a world as we would wish it to be.

Reflection of this sort is about more than objectivity—it's about trusting our passions and feelings too. George Orwell wrote that all good writing was political and to some extent even egotistical. If we take the generous interpretation of those terms then I tend to agree. Writing for me has a purpose. I want to influence change for the good. But I also want to help others make better and more informed choices in the circumstances they encounter. For all that I draw heavily on my own experience, it's not really about me at all. It's about all of us and the paths—however uncertain—that we imagine we might take.

THE FAIR VALUE EQUATION

NOT FAR FROM MY London house is the Charles Dickens museum, a three-story Georgian terrace where the author chronicled the life and poverty of Victorian England. From here it's a short walk to many of his novels' famous settings: Smithfield Market, the Old Curiosity Shop, and the now repurposed workhouses that were once a commonplace feature of the city.

We have come a long way in improving the social conditions that inspired novels like *Oliver Twist*. Indeed, it's said that were it ever possible to return to those times, a modern-day visitor would be traumatized not only by the sights—but by what they would smell! The sanitary conditions of London were so poor that for several summers in the 1850s it was described as the Great Stink.

Imagine for a moment what that must have been like—not in Dickens's comfortable home, but in the filth and hopelessness of the slums which surrounded it. Imagine too, the bass note of fear that accompanied a life without health care, decent education, or fair access to the law—where the refuge of last resort was the workhouse, a fate so dreadful that only the desperate ever entered.

It's sobering to think that these conditions existed at a time of relative peace and prosperity, in what was then the most powerful nation on earth.

That they were tolerated was not so much for want of resources, but as a lack of empathy with those who suffered the consequences. Questions of fairness and value were regarded as matters of charity or evangelism rather than deriving from our fundamental rights or the duties of a compassionate state. The dominant social ethic of the time was framed by the idea of the *deserving and underserving poor*, a belief (from those with power and privilege) that we flourish or fail through our efforts and industry alone.

Such views are now rightly seen as naive, but we are far from abandoning them. Indeed, since the dismantling of the USSR and the reinvention of China, the western capitalist model of meritocratic enterprise has relegated more egalitarian alternatives to the fringes. And in many ways, that's a good thing—for it's evidentially true that industry and incentive reap both individual and collective reward.

The difference today is that we understand the race of opportunity is far from fair—that while our endeavors make a difference, our starting point has a significant bearing on the progress we are likely to make. This is why we have free and universal education, why we outlaw discrimination, why children are protected from poverty. Modern day meritocracy recognizes that in a world where rewards are unequally spread, the competition for them should be as equitable as possible—at least, that's the theory!

In practice, we all know that inequality, and the burdens that come with it, is still rife. We know too, that while there is no merit in being born into money, wealth and success follow hand-in-hand, just as surely as social mobility is the devil's only job for those without privilege. The pursuit of what the philosopher John Rawles called "true equality of opportunity" remains a work in progress, albeit that most developed nations have a positive trajectory.

In sharing these thoughts, I'm deeply conscious that I have fared especially well in the lottery of life's chances. I like to think that ambition and ability have played their part, but it's impossible to deny the blessings I've had. Psychologists tell us that a significant determiner of our prospects can be something as simple as being read bedtime stories as a child—I came from a house full of books and a family that encouraged me to study; that alone is priceless. I also benefited from an enlightened system of social welfare that provided me with education, health care, and, ultimately, a choice of roads to travel that are a world away from the dead-ends of nineteenth century London.

Today, I spend much of my time commuting between the US and Europe. Both are wonderful societies in their way—and we should largely rejoice in what they've achieved. But if there's a single difference between my experience of people's lives in these two economic powerhouses, it's the prevalence of a residual anxiety that is rooted in inadequate social provision for large numbers in American communities. The most common question my European friends ask me—invariably with a sense of incredulity—is why the US, the richest and most powerful nation on earth, is so reluctant to provide universal, free to access healthcare?

It's not my purpose—or my place—to delve too deeply into politics. The reference to health care is more a reporting of the transatlantic attitudinal differences than any polemic on my part. Rather, I'm reflecting on how our collective values have impacts that go so much deeper than our fiscal systems and the scope of the services our governments provide. I call this the *fair value equation*, measuring the worth of our society in terms not only of what it produces but also the compassion it shows and the wellbeing that results.

Business has much to teach us here. The reflection above might imply there is conflict between the two goals, but in practice we know the best companies have the most progressive policies, treat their people with care, show concern for the environment . . . It's no coincidence that there are few organizations of size that operate today without a clear statement of values.

And furthermore, it's no surprise that those organizations which found their policies on "true equality of opportunity" have the highest levels of engagement. This isn't because they pay higher wages, for the relationship between remuneration and employee commitment is weak. True engagement—and the discretionary effort which follows—comes from a combination of involvement, progression, fair and equitable treatment, and, most importantly of all, a commonly held belief that everyone is a fully valued member of the organization, regardless of their seniority.

Returning to our governments, if as societies we provide less than is necessary for citizens to feel they have a fair stake in their communities, then we should expect engagement of a different sort. History shows us that the biggest threats to our democracies and freedom have come from those who feel excluded—in the despair which follows, it's all too easy to be persuaded by simplistic solutions that play to our survival instincts. The roots of fascism, nationalism, and what today we call populism, lie not in a rational assessment of our best interests, but a sense of hopelessness and the fear which comes with it.

In Northern and Western Europe, the socio-political model is based (significantly more so than the US) on the provision of universal public services, underpinned by a wide-reaching safety net that, if not exactly eliminating, at least dulls that bass note of anxiety I spoke of earlier. Counter to nineteenth century thinking, the result is not any loss of incentive or productivity from those at the bottom of the social ladder. Indeed, the countries with the most comprehensive welfare systems have the highest levels of intergenerational social mobility. Meanwhile the US, far from being the land of opportunity, has one of the poorest records in this regard.

Enlightened leadership doesn't mean there are no hierarchies, or that remuneration and reward should be equally spread. But it does mean we must recognize the pursuit of success is a joint endeavor, and that we flourish most when we nurture the prospects of all. If—on the contrary—we exclude sections of our workforce, deny them fair opportunity, or provide only insecure contracts—then we lose out on their full potential.

In practice then, the two sides of the fair value equation operate not in conflict but in concert. If our care lacks depth, then commitment will be shallow—but so too the opposite, and therein lies our opportunity.

Pursuing this alternative course can require a leap of faith—not least because there will always be some who seek to game the system. But I'd argue this is a small price to pay. For the alternative is not so much a race to the bottom as a burden that weighs us down as individuals and societies.

To lighten the load, we need surely to share it—not as a penance, but in the knowledge that unless we do so, gravity will win, and all of us are diminished as a consequence.

We might be mindful too of the fates of Mr. and Mrs. Bumble, the workhouse-keepers in *Oliver Twist*. Their hearts were said to be impervious to tears; 'waterproof' is how Dickens' described them. But as the story, and their pursuit of self-interest, unfolds, they "were gradually reduced to great indigence and misery, and finally became paupers in that very same workhouse in which they had once lorded it over others."

GATHERING

GATHERING — A MEETING PLACE OF
PEOPLE & IDEAS; OF LEAVES
BOUND TOGETHER IN A BOOK.

To believe your own thought, to believe that what is true for you in your private heart is true for all men,—that is genius. Speak your latent conviction, and it shall be the universal sense; for the inmost in due time becomes the outmost.

Ralph Waldo Emerson

THE VALUE OF VIRTUES

THE ANCIENT PHILOSOPHER ARISTOTLE understood a thing or two about how to achieve success. According to his writings, a good and satisfying life was one that navigated a course between the extremes of hedonism and deficiency. And the way to do this, he asserted, was by living in accordance with our *virtues*—those qualities and behaviors that we all, universally, recognize as *good*, and which, in his view, were best nurtured by experience and daily practice rather than prescriptive rules.

Fast forward more than two thousand years and *virtue theory* is enjoying something of a well-deserved renaissance, most notably through the positive psychology movement and the writings of Martin Seligman. Its relevance to business is gaining traction too, and justifiably so, because the virtue theory adds a layer to our understanding of that other *V* word, *V* for values, which has evolved into a ubiquitous concept in the progressive workplace.

There are few organizations today that would fail to acknowledge the importance of values. The idea that an engaged workforce, aligned to the goals of the company and working with common principles, helps to drive performance, is not only common sense, it is backed by a raft of evidence which crosses sectors, cultures, and continents. Whether formalized or not, the best performing organizations across the globe have strong value sets which underpin their culture and provide a sense of meaning and belonging to their people.

But if the awareness of values is now commonplace, the concept of virtues remains somewhat academic, even though its benefits are just as transformational and equally self-evident.

By virtues, we mean those personal qualities that all of us recognize as beneficial to ourselves, others, and the community at large. In his work on positive psychology, Seligman identifies several high-level categories such as courage, wisdom, humanity, and justice. Beneath these are more tangible qualities such as creativity, diligence, fairness, and teamwork. In all, he lists twenty-four strengths that are universally recognized as positive attributes and contribute to a collective good. While each of us has a preference and greater capacity for some virtues over others, all of us are happiest and most satisfied when we are able to employ these positive characteristics in our day-to-day lives.

It's not necessary to dig deep into philosophy or psychology to take some lessons from this. For leaders and professionals, the critical point is that we all give our best and make our greatest contribution when the work we do supports our positive motivations. Consequently, if we can align roles and responsibilities across our organizations—and provide opportunities that nurture the virtues—then both our colleagues and our businesses are more likely to flourish. Having clear values helps us to establish the rules and guidelines for common behaviors; promoting virtues goes a level deeper, encouraging our individual strengths for the collective good.

I like to think of living by our virtues as the difference between *being in a rut* and *ploughing one's own furrow.* In the former, we are trapped in a cycle of activity that feels meaningless and lacks personal satisfaction—even if the organization and its goals are worthy, we as individuals don't fit, because the role we are asked to play doesn't have room for those qualities that motivate and self-propel us. By contrast, in following a path which plays well to our individual strengths, we give and achieve more, thereby benefiting ourselves and our wider community. To use a sporting analogy: how often do we hear soccer coaches talking of the need to give creative players *the freedom to express themselves*—in a sense, that is virtue theory in action.

In a workplace setting, promoting virtues can be as simple as allowing a few hours a week for more lateral thinking (*creativity and curiosity*), or offering the opportunity for development training (*love of learning*); it might mean shaping a job to include more group activities (*teamwork*) or allowing colleagues to self-organize charitable activities (*social awareness, kindness*). In truth, much of this, good leaders do instinctively, encouraging something similar in wider organizational goals. Though they might not use the term *virtue theory*, many of its key elements are inherent to contemporary thinking on issues such as diversity and inclusion—valuing differences and allowing us all to give the best of ourselves.

There's relevance in virtue theory for our corporate strategies too. In the courting stage, contemplated acquisitions and mergers almost invariably sweeten the numbers, estimating the potential for synergies, market share, pricing power, and other benefits. And yet so much of this M&A activity ultimately fails to deliver the intended results. By applying the lens of *virtue theory*, we might consider more carefully whether the acquirer will be a good parent or partner; are its organizational virtues compatible or in conflict with those of its target?

And finally, as individuals navigating our career paths, the idea of living in harmony with our strengths and preferences is an invaluable perspective when viewing our situation and prospects. Seligman describes the pursuit of virtues as the "gold standard of human well-being," the root of the positive choices we make in our efforts to flourish. At times, that may involve difficult choices—and I recognize that the freedom to act varies by circumstance—but across a career or a lifetime, finding your niche, feeling energized and ready for the day, undeniably is worth some sacrifice. For as Aristotle claimed many centuries ago, there is no one prescription for success, but being true to our positive natures is the surest route to follow.

FEAR AND THE
PRICE TAG OF TRUST

AS A YOUNG BOY growing up in Peer, it was natural I'd want to learn to ride a bike. For though Belgium is not awash with heroes, we had all heard of Eddy Merckx, widely regarded as the world's greatest cyclist. The problem, at least at first, was that I wasn't very good. No sooner would I start pedaling than I'd panic and crash to the ground. After yet another painful tumble, my father once exclaimed, "The problem is, you're so afraid of falling, that you forget to push through."

Fear, of course, can be both physical and mental. In acutely stressful situations, we trigger hormones that have their evolutionary root in our ancestral environment. When faced with danger, our bodies tell us to either fight, flee, or freeze. The symptoms include heart palpitations, sweaty palms, and the need to pee! Psychologically, our attention is drawn to the immediate, our focus narrows, and we act according to our instincts rather than any deeper reasoning.

I sometimes wonder if there's a political equivalent. In the US, as I write, the nation is in the midst of the Trump-Biden presidential campaigns. The anxiety is palpable and, in many ways, more so than any policy differences. Rustbelt America dreads the return of an out of touch elite; the graduates of Boston abhor what they read on Twitter; our banks are concerned about a move to the Left; our destitute remain fearful of the Right. It comes to something when even the postal system has been politicized for fear of fraud in what's regarded as the home of freedom.

Something similar is happening in the UK. The issue of Brexit has paralyzed British politics for the last five years, and arguably longer. Business is disrupted, investment delayed, uncertainty and mistrust are endemic. Despite a referendum and a general election, there is no sign of a consensus that might unite the nation in a common endeavor. The schism between those who would fight and those who would flee is as divisive and draining as ever.

Imagine if we were to run business this way—if there were no requirement to balance the interests of stakeholders but rather to meet only the needs of those who held most sway. Such a model would tear our companies apart, destroying value for all through the pursuit of a blinkered agenda. If I have learned anything as an organizational leader, it's that sustainable progress requires a broader and longer-range perspective than the hollow promises of trouble-shooters and partisans.

This is not to say that decisive action is never required—procrastination can be as deadly as impetuousness. But it is to assert that good business must do more—and better—than to decide by majority or follow homogenous agendas. That's why diversity is so important. We thrive, and make better decisions, by considering a variety of perspectives; by ensuring we have not only social, ethnic, and gender balance in our teams, but something of the same in our modes of thinking—we need creatives and disruptors, just as much as we need hard-nosed operators and cautious finance directors.

The historian Niall Ferguson has spoken of the lack of empathy in contemporary political debate, as if putting ourselves in someone else's shoes is to concede the unthinkable, to legitimize the *other* who threatens our sense of safety. Ferguson is an erudite academic, a Stanford fellow who must cringe at the gaucheness or superficiality of any populist political agenda. And yet, perhaps more than any other commentator, he has sought to understand and communicate its appeal, acknowledging that while populist leaders have a loose relationship to facts, they also call out truths that are deeply felt by many. His theme is not that these are noble politicians, but that unless we allow ourselves to look beyond their rhetoric—and acknowledge the concerns that underlie their appeal—we will not make progress together. We need to listen and try to understand the views and concerns of others than ourselves, even if we are convinced that they are "wrong."

To be this generous is difficult. My response to the political decisions I perceive as foolish or unjust ranges from anger to despair —and especially so when there is a disingenuity to those delivering the message. In a sense, it's a cognitive equivalent of the fight or flight phenomenon. My values tell me there are lines we must not cross, and on these, I am firm. But I know also that politics is not an ethical exercise—that what *is* weighs more heavily than what *ought*—and that the pursuit of power has its own self-rationalizing dynamic. To expect better of our leaders is better held as a hope than an expectation.

Hope, nonetheless, is a powerful counterforce to the problems of the present. It's why all leaders trade on vision and why those in business must do likewise—though ideally, with more veracity and sincerity than their political counterparts. Vision—in the sense of laying out a positive future for our companies—is in many ways what modern leadership is most about. To succeed, we must bring others with us, keep our word, and win the trust of more than a slim majority.

The cost of fear—or, put differently, the price-tag of trust—is intangibly vast. In football management the term to "lose the dressing room" means to have lost the confidence of your players. It invariably ends in tears. After the financial crash, our banks spent millions of dollars revisiting their values—a decade later, they are still to convince us. The police and other public bodies are under similar pressure— Black Lives Matter is but one example of injustices that are deeply felt by those who've lost faith.

When our fears are most immediate—and most beyond our control—we seek salvation in simplicity. That's why in any financial crash, the demand for gilts and gold will rise—a "rush to quality" is what it's known as. We look to authority too, whether that be through prayers or deference to hierarchies that compensate for our feelings of impotence. Salvation means, literally, to be saved from ruin—it strikes me, the appeal of populist politics is something similar.

In certain situations, this approach may be appropriate. When faced with a hurricane, most of us know it's best to follow the advice of the experts. But to resolve more complex problems and overcome discord that is deeply rooted, we must look beyond simplistic panaceas. We must pool our knowledge and ideas, and have the courage, as leaders, to give way to the wisdom of others. To overcome fear, we must find what unites us before addressing what divides.

In his magnificent book, *Sapiens: a brief history of humankind*, Yuval Noah Hurari chronicles the progress of humanity. Eschewing the usual chronology of princes and kings, he examines how, as a species, we have made such remarkable progress—reflecting on what it is about our abilities and psychology that has taken us from a few hundred thousand to eight billion individuals. And at root, his answer lies in our ability to work flexibly together, using language and reasoning to keep faith with ideas that bind us in common causes—be those money, nation states, laws—and, more recently in historical terms, companies and international institutions.

I take strength from his long-term perspective. Not only in the stoic maxim of "this too will pass," but in the knowledge that regressive periods, such as the one in which I believe we're currently mired, are blips on the curve. There are more millennials in China than the entire population of the United States—no amount of retrenchment will resist that commercial imperative, and the opportunities it brings. We are, on the whole, freer today than we have ever been; we are less likely to die from conflict, have longer life expectancy, better education... Many of our deepest fears are trivial compared to those our forefathers took in their stride.

There are exceptions to this optimism—the climate crisis is perhaps the most obvious—and we shouldn't live on the basis that "all will be well in the Twenty-second Century." But as I learned as a boy, the surest way to fall from a bike is to focus only on the wheel in front of you. To make collective progress—be that in business, politics, or as people—we must have faith in our future, a care for each other, and a trust that extends beyond tomorrow.

My father was wrong when he said I wasn't pushing through—the problem was that I wasn't looking far enough ahead.

WHY TRUST MATTERS IN THE WORKPLACE, AND WHY WE SHOULD CARE

ACROSS MUCH OF THE developed world, faith in institutions is rupturing. Modern day politics, with a regrettable tendency to provide impulsive, populistic solutions to problems of extreme complexity, contributes to an undercurrent of skepticism, which in turn feeds further unease and polarization, undermining confidence. In a host of democracies, leadership is variously described as broken, dysfunctional, and unrepresentative. Little wonder then, that survey after survey reveals public trust to be at all-time low.

Regardless of one's political opinions—passions even—this is deeply corrosive. For trust is essential to positive human relationships and one of the most valuable tools in building progressive societies. Without it there can be no exchange, no collective endeavor, no promises relied on, and worse, no dreams shared or secrets confided. Trust, in its broadest sense, is so ubiquitous that we seldom give it a thought. And yet, a moment's reflection reveals its criticality to all that we are and achieve together.

There are obvious parallels to the business environment. It will be no surprise that trust is the single most important value associated with successful brands. When we're working together in our businesses, we count on each other as surely as mountaineers rely on their partners to hold the rope. In my current organization—along with thousands more—we call out trust as a core value in our working practices, our relations with customers, and care for each other.

And that word *care* seems essential to maximizing trust's potential. We can cooperate with individuals and institutions for their utility—because, through experience, we have learned there is more to be won than lost—and we should never diminish the importance of this fact. But to view trust entirely as a profitable exchange, risks turning it into a sort of game theory, a slightly Machiavellian approach in which we weigh up possibilities and strategize to maximize our advantage.

Trust as care is something infinitely more powerful.

To trust because we care not only for the outcome, but also for the person or the process, creates a deeper and stronger bond. When a master craftsman gives his trust to a young apprentice, he's saying something that no invoice or profit and loss account ever could. And what's more, the trainee knows it too! All of us who are business professionals will have experienced equivalent moments and be able to recall the boost to our self-esteem, and the growth in confidence it gave us.

Confidence, of course, is intimately linked to trust. Search any thesaurus and the two words will be listed side by side, along with faith, reliance, dependence. But trust is a verb as well as a noun. In trusting, we make an active choice, the exercise of which is essential to allow others (and ourselves) to flourish. In other words, trust is something we give; confidence—and all that comes with it—is what is received.

Institutions and organizations ignore this insight at their peril. For no matter how attractive the alternatives may seem, in the long run, people care if their politicians lie, if their faith leaders are hypocrites, if the media invents its own news. And for those of us in mainstream commerce, the lesson is much the same. Customers no longer judge a business only by its products; they want to know how well we treat our people, whether we act responsibly, and if we pay our taxes.

In a mirror image of the virtuous circle I described earlier, if companies fail to engage with these concerns, then trust will be withheld, and belief will die in its turn.

Simon Sinek's recent book, *The Infinite Game,* talks of the need for leaders to trust and care beyond the moment. Millennials—who soon will represent 50 percent of the workforce—are long-term thinkers; they want to belong and contribute to meaningful roles, and they want to work in cultures that allow for self-expression, that value their contribution, and allow for risk-taking without fear of retribution. Leaders, Sinek asserts, have a special responsibility to set the tone in creating an atmosphere of trust and cooperation.

While Sinek's position is something I believe we can intuitively subscribe to, it doesn't require a management guru for us to learn this simple truth. Most of us know, as a matter of common sense and experience, that when teams show trust and care—when colleagues have each other's back—then performance, motivation, and retention surely follow. Just as we know that organizations which fail to nurture their people will lose talent, commitment, and, ultimately, any meaningful purpose.

Furthermore, I'd argue it doesn't require formal authority to make a difference. Whatever our circumstance or seniority, individual actions can and do have an impact. We can give trust—and show we care—by something as simple as passing the ball, waiting our turn, or listening respectfully to a colleague's opinion. Trust, as we experience it, is a bi-lateral transaction—all it needs to flourish is two people, doing the right thing, by and for each other.

And hopefully we can all agree that a world with more trust is a better and more joyful place.

WHY COMPANIES MAKE HARMFUL DECISIONS

WHY IS IT THAT companies make bad decisions?

In posing that question, I'm not referring to those infamous bad calls like Decca record's rejection of The Beatles, or Blockbuster's rebuff of a joint venture with Netflix. These are human mistakes—and with the benefit of hindsight, we can, all of us, believe we'd have made a smarter choice.

Rather, what interests me is why, given all the checks and balances, so many companies appear to take carefully thought through decisions that actively harm the interests of their stakeholders.

A Harvard Business Report estimated that up to 90 percent of all mergers and acquisitions fail; similar claims can be made for internal transformation projects, especially in the IT and digital sphere. Whatever way you look at the problem, it seems that despite access to the smartest minds, sophisticated forecasting tools, and due diligence warnings, business leaders continue to get it wrong.

Observation has taught me there's no single explanation. But after twenty years of corporate decision making—and with the scars to prove it—I've at least become attentive to some of the warning signs.

What follows are therefore my insights from experience. Interpret them as you wish, for every situation will be different, which leads nicely to my first observation, that gets straight to the root of the problem.

COMPLEXITY

The unfortunate reality is that many strategic decisions are not as binary as whether or not to award a recording contract. Rather, they are multifaceted, involving forecasts of markets, competitors, savings, and synergies. And what's more, many of the situations are particular to circumstance, so references are seldom available or even helpful if they were.

In these sorts of complex situations, we all—and organizations are no different—resort to simplified solutions that allow for a quicker way through the maze. Academics call these heuristics—we know them as *rules of thumb, best estimates, benchmarking,* and the like.

The trouble with heuristics is that although they are to some extent inevitable, we risk addressing a simpler problem than the one we face—and worse, our biases and preferences creep into the proposed solution to issues that have been framed for our convenience rather than the reality of the situation.

One antidote—so far as any is effective—is to be extremely careful when simplifying or estimating significant variables. Any benchmarks we chose and assumptions we make, must also be modeled over a wide range of outcomes. The greatest danger of heuristics is actually a regression to the mean, where risks and opportunities are smoothed into a safe bet, which in the event, turns out to be anything but.

IMPULSIVENESS

Linked to our tendency to simplify, is a pressure to act—fueled by a deeply ingrained corporate mindset that regards not doing so as a missed opportunity or cultural failing. Organizations increasingly demand that their leaders move at pace, and while this has its benefits, it can also lead to premature decisions that are ahead of the curve.

In transformational projects, the term *bleeding edge* refers to the impact of decisions—typically those involving the early adoption of technology—which lead to unexpected costs and consequences that in turn harm rather than enhance competitiveness. The underlying reason is that the supposed "first-mover advantage" inevitably comes with significantly greater risks. In almost any sizable market, the lesson of case study after case study is that a little more patience would often have led to a better outcome.

To some extent, this is as much an institutional as an individual problem. I often sense that companies weigh the *regret risk* of missed opportunities more heavily than they do the years of successful delivery. Investors—like sports fans—are both impatient for success and quick to point out the triumphs of others. What they are less good at doing is recognizing the potential for pitfalls and giving due regard to the judgment of those who avoid them.

There is no cure-all solution to impulsiveness, but it is good practice to ensure decisions can be made over sensible timeframes, to resist the pressure to lead on every front, and to establish agreed expectations for investment and return over time—and then stick to them!

REWARD VERSUS RISK

At the heart of the type of decisions we're discussing is the assessment of risk versus reward.

Of course, no opportunity of any consequence is a certainty—investors, colleagues, and customers all understand that. It's also fair to say that most successful executives need to be less risk-averse than say, librarians. But while that's a good thing, my experience is that risk and reward assessments are often made in a manner which gives undue weight to one over the other.

Think for a moment of all those inspirational quotes you've seen at management conferences: "Whatever you dream, begin it—for boldness has power and magic!" (Goethe); "Security is mostly superstition . . ."

(Hellen Keller); "Do not fear mistakes; there are none!" (Miles Davis)

Extracts like these can be fine as a means to inspire a sales team or encourage creativity, but their underlying message can—and in my experience often does—contribute to a mindset which lionizes risk taking.

I'm not suggesting that the potted wisdom of Miles Davis is taken too literally by senior executives. But when it comes to major strategic decisions, the notion that boldness equates to virtue remains a powerful force, and a significant hindrance to a full and objective assessment of downside consequences.

THE DREAM OF REASON

We should also recognize that objectivity is more of an attitude than a destination we ever arrive at. The belief that we can accurately predict the future through analysis and situational modeling alone has been the downfall of many an economist—or for that matter politician.

In practice, we live in a less than rational, often emotional, and certainly disruptive world—companies and organizations can never fully predict the response of others, or indeed, the impact of change on their people and its consequent effect on a multitude of other factors. Which is why softer considerations are vital.

CULTURE AND COMMUNICATIONS

In analyzing harmful decisions, the diagnosis often points less to the actions we have taken, than the way we went about them.

For example, bringing together two organizations might seem straightforward on paper, but as with personal relationships, there's more to a good match than aligning compatible skills and qualities. Too many mergers are predicated on the assumption that the mores of one party can be imposed on the other—giving scant regard to the importance of culture, communication, and values as drivers of performance.

Successful ventures pay attention to these softer qualities, avoiding the imposition of changes that are diametrically opposed to the past, or rewarding individuals with extended remits for which they have little understanding.

The same cultural empathy should apply to our search for synergies, sales growth, or even colleague engagement—we should not assume that crashing together, or worse, imposing one style on the other, will bring success.

Think Borg and McEnroe—both exceptional tennis players, but at the height of their career, not the most compatible doubles pairing.

IMBALANCE OF STAKEHOLDERS

This understanding of partnership is never more important than in the balance of stakeholder interests. All commercial organizations have at least three key constituencies: their investors, employees, and customers. And while all of these will want the company to prosper, they each have subtly different needs and emphases.

Successful organizations make decisions in a way that ensures all stakeholders take a fair share of the risks and rewards. This means investors accepting there are other calls on cash than paying dividends, employees understanding that job security comes from embracing change, and customers having realistic expectations on price and value despite the leverage they may have.

Conversely, if the interests of one stakeholder group begin to dominate, it can be a green light to harmful decision making. Over the lifecycle of a business, there will, of course, be times of different emphasis—but on the whole, sustainable decisions are founded on meeting the needs of each constituency, while avoiding the ascendancy of any.

AND FINALLY . . .

I could go on with a host of other reasons . . .

But I'm conscious there's a limit to the value of observations from experience, and particularly aware that hindsight makes prophets of us all—or in my case, the best Monday morning quarterback to never grace the field.

Perhaps the most important thing, in seeking to understand why so many companies make harmful choices, is to recognize it's not the corporate entity that makes those decisions at all—it is people!

And, as human beings, we are all in equal part blessed and susceptible to the paradoxical mix of talents, frailties, and hubris that drive our exceptional achievements as well as our greatest mistakes.

GIVING TO OTHERS—AND OF OURSELVES

THE FACE LOOKING AT me from the newspaper is perhaps six years old. It's a young boy in a makeshift tent, mud on his cheeks, hands clasped as if in prayer. The caption tells me he's lost his home, and that winter may take his life. I think it's his eyes that move me most, speaking of a horror that no child should bear. My palms feel sticky as I pick up the phone, text HELP, and make a donation to the Syrian refugee appeal.

Fundraisers like these have become part of the fabric of our lives—they are in our magazines, on TV, even posters on the subway. So commonplace are these images that we learn to filter them out. In the newspaper I was reading, there were similar appeals for cancer research, wildlife conservation, homelessness, and victims of domestic abuse. At times, it seems there's no end to the call on our goodwill.

And that should not be surprising, for the urge to alleviate suffering is surely part of our humanity. Indeed, to have no sympathy for the pain of others is a mark of a psychopath. And yet we cannot credibly respond to every cry for help. In the United States, there are estimated to be 1.5 million registered nonprofit organizations and in the UK around a third of that number, with similar proliferation of social ventures across the developed world.

This "third sector," as it's sometimes called, has become a significant part of our social infrastructure and, in many ways, it's as competitive for our attentions as the mainstream economy. We choose our causes and, from the natural disorder of what is effectively a *market for our hearts*, there emerges a growing wealth of charity in the broadest and most generous sense of that term. Or so the theory goes.

The notion of charity as the desire to eliminate suffering is sometimes contrasted to a broader vision of philanthropy and the quest to find lasting solutions for the root causes of our problems. We tend to think of philanthropists as a rich few, often historical figures with a social conscience. In liberal democracies, much of their role is now given over to the state, with nonprofits filling the gaps and addressing more immediate and particular needs.

To my mind, the distinction is somewhat academic. All of us are aware that the problems in Syria or Somalia—or even our neighborhood—are the result of forces which ought to be fixed. But we also know that hungry bellies need feeding and traumatized children will not survive winter in a tent. Those caught in the crosswinds of circumstance are deserving of both our immediate attention and our efforts to make greater and longer lasting change.

And, mostly, the two approaches go hand in hand. Very few larger charities are focused only on the here and now, and yet, understandably, they will seek to leverage our more visceral responses to raise funds and build awareness—just as they will lobby the rich and famous, be they individuals, governments, or corporations, for larger donations that offer the promise (and reflected aura) of a legacy difference.

But for many of us, all of this can seem somewhat removed. Which is surely why so many smaller organizations still thrive in the face of what's become a quasi-corporate competition for our sympathies. A remark often misattributed to Winston Churchill is, "We make a living by what we get, but make a life by what we give." It nonetheless contains the truth which lies behind our desire not only to donate cash, which—good though that it is—can feel like conscience appeasement, but to volunteer and campaign for causes, which—although they may seem peripheral to others—are closest to our hearts.

I recall a colleague complaining to me, not unkindly but in frustration, about the fundraisers at his local school. They were so inefficient, he said; hours spent baking cakes and running raffles, when frankly if everyone who cared had simply donated twenty dollars, they'd have raised twice as much in half the time. He was probably right, but of course he misses the point of the exercise. We get our children involved in community work as much for the lessons it teaches them as the difference they can tangibly make.

Of course, the definition of community is wider now than ever. For some it remains rooted in their neighborhood, their church, or school. For others, that sense of belonging might come from their workplace, their hobbies, or their ethnicity. This is a good thing, for the diversity of interests leads ultimately to richer lives for us all and, I would argue, a voluntary sector that better reflects our needs and concerns than any interventionist design could hope to do. Which is why, wearing my corporate hat for a moment, we should resist calls for overregulation of the nonprofit sector.

Instead, we should encourage involvement and giving of different sorts—awarding tax breaks and stipends to those who volunteer, for example—and promoting new models of contribution that draw on our collective efforts as well as our cash. Throughout my career, I've had the privilege to work with many gifted individuals and have seen the progress that their flair makes possible. It's common for the leaders of many different faiths to ask their followers to gift a percentage of their income, but consider the impact if all of us offered a percentage of our talents. For some that might mean baking cakes—and it's good that they do—but for an academic say, it could be directing a percentage of their research at social issues, or for executives like myself, advising on strategies and governance.

In the US and the UK, nonprofits are typically seen as a substitute to state funding, but there are other approaches that we can learn from. I've already mentioned the roles of the churches and faiths, which are prominent in many cultures. Across much of mainland Europe there is often a more social-corporate model, with close cooperation and even contracting between the state and charities. In Scandinavia and the Netherlands, where high taxes and high-quality services are the norm, the emphasis is on volunteering and participation.

The pool of our talent is limitless, and it is here, I believe, where the potential for a modern philanthropy lies. Lasting social solutions are seldom designed from above, rather they evolve through an iterative process of progress and refinement, underpinned by care for the outcome. This asks more of us than the adverts and appeals that surround us, and requires leaders to step forward and encourage others to do the same. But here's the thing: it pays us back in spades. Short of utopia, there will always be a role for larger organizations, and thank goodness they are there. But to have a wider, more caring society, we need to bridge the gap between ourselves and those in need with something more tangible than simply texting HELP.

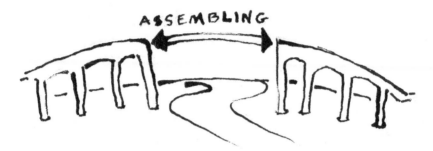

ASSEMBLING

A COMING TOGETHER OF
CONSTITUENT PARTS - FIT FOR A PURPOSE.

It is our choice of good or evil that determines our character, not our opinion about good or evil. [. . .] Excellence is never an accident. It is always the result of high intention, sincere effort, and intelligent execution; it represents the wise choice of many alternatives . . .

Aristotle

REFLECTIONS ON DOHA

AS I WRITE THIS essay, the eyes of the world's press are focused on Doha and its hosting of the World Athletics Championships. Here in the UK, interest has been intense. Dinah Asher Smith's victory in the 200 meters was a masterclass of controlled and specialized technique, but it was Katerina Johnson Thompson's gold in the heptathlon that caught my eye—and not because she beat a Belgian into second place.

The heptathlon is one of the ultimate trials of all-round athletic ability. From shot-put to sprinting, the discipline tests speed, strength, and stamina, as well as the mental power to hold it all together over two days of competition. In contrast to Asher Smith's twenty seconds of brilliance, Johnson Thompson's victory required a balance of skills, none of them world-beating on their own, but which, collectively, others could not match.

Since returning to the UK as CEO of a large distributor, I've been impressed by a similar quality in our distribution business. Handling an average of five million products every day, it delivers to 27,000 outlets from superstores to corner shops, collecting unsold goods, processing data to forecast demand, taking customer calls, invoicing, and all of it achieved in the tightest of time windows.

And yet, if we examine the unique skills of news wholesaling, what we find is that success more resembles a heptathlon than a sprint. What underpins our competitiveness is not so much that we are very best at physical or even time sensitive delivery, nor are we peerless leaders in information management, invoicing, or customer services. Rather, we are *good* at all these things, and it is this optimum combination of our arguably suboptimal parts that makes us world class at what we do.

That's not to say there isn't room for improvement. As with athletics, standards move on, expectations increase, and the competition is always at our shoulders. As leaders and strategists, the lesson from this week's heptathlon in Doha, is that we must take a holistic view, considering the impact of each initiative in its wider context—ensuring the strength we build in one area doesn't sap our speed or stamina in another.

It strikes me that the metaphor of "leader as coach" is never more apt than in complex and well-established organizations—not least because the catalogue of good companies brought down by supposedly transformative projects should give us pause for thought. But that pause must never lead to indecision.

The danger in managing this type of complexity is that answers can tend towards those that start with "*but.*" As leaders, we must accept that all decisions involve some risk, including the choice to leave matters alone. Risk can feel uncomfortable, threatening even, but a failure to commit is the surest way to ensure the competition will soon be pressing at your heels.

Making progress, while limiting our exposure, requires that we draw on analysis as well as experience; creativity balanced by objective measures, and occasionally some counter-intuitive thinking. Standard operating procedures, for example, might appear to be a restrictor to change, but we should view them more as athletes see solid technique. For only when we have sound and consistent foundations can we test and, most importantly, measure the impact of changes we might introduce. In a world where all the parts are different, it's tough to know what works, what doesn't, or what to do next.

If I were to add one more ingredient, it would be to encourage, and be seen to exercise, appropriate humility. For no one can be right all the time and not every idea will be a success. Occasionally—though hopefully not too often—we must hold up our hands and learn from the experience. It is not being wrong that we should fear, it is being too proud to change course when the evidence is clear.

Returning to Doha, in the time I've drafted this piece, the UK teams have won silver medals in both the sprint relays—the men pipped, I might add, by the Americans, if not the Belgians! The relay of course is all about passing the baton, with success being more than the sum of the parts. That's a subject for another day, but it reminds me that harnessing the commitment of our teams to a bold but measurable strategy, is the best way to exceed our expectations.

DISRUPTION AS THE NEW NORMAL

DISRUPTION!

THERE MUST BE FEW words more likely to provoke unease among executives and investors alike. Almost universally, the term is used in the negative sense by the mainstream; its very mention associated with disturbance, upset, and impediment . . .

Yet its incidence is on the rise, as evidenced by any number of surveys predicting that the majority of listed businesses will face market disorder in the next five years—as well as a raft of statistical studies, confirming a grim toll of companies that have already succumbed.

In a business context, disruption is an innovation or intervention which changes a market pattern, creating new value chains that typically undermine the established profitability of incumbents. That's why it's so feared by those who might at first appear to be the most able to resist. Over the last twenty years, we've all witnessed, and most likely contributed to, the reshaping of once stable industries which proves these concerns are well-founded; the rise of online retail and the demise of many brick-and-mortar giants is an obvious example.

But it would be a mistake to regard the problem as particular to— or exclusively caused by—the digital and technology sectors. That's because market disruption is ultimately a process, not a *thing*—its defining characteristic is the reimagining of the status quo, with ideas that take root in niche opportunities and later come to challenge the establishment.

And here lies the critical importance of leadership in responding to what is undoubtedly one of the biggest challenges of our time. By seeing disruption in terms of method and mindset, we can regain the initiative and turn a feared externality into a constructive force for good.

The American writer and thinker Robert Pirsig (most famous for *Zen and the Art of Motorcycle Maintenance*) suggested that all systems evolve their worth in two distinct ways. Firstly, through periods of *static quality*, in which they work to maximize the efficiency and productivity of established processes. And secondly, through occasional periods of *dynamic quality* in which that order is radically disrupted and new norms are established. These step-changes, he claimed, are invariably sparked by the mavericks, shamans, and outsiders who see things through a different lens.

The consequences for senior leaders are far from simple to address. How do we best manage these two dynamics, embracing the need for change without destroying the value of what we already have? And how do we balance the need for experience and incremental efficiency, with the innovation and fresh thinking that's essential for a future we can't yet see?

It's important to recognize that not all disruption is revolutionary, or even of the sort typified by internet start-ups, where *not to be first is to be last*. Over the next decade, developments such as Big Data, Artificial Intelligence, and environmentalism will move more slowly but, in the long run, they are likely to cause even greater transformations across many more sectors. Consider, for example, the potential impact of 5G and the Internet of Things, not only on manufacturing but on customer experience, data analytics, education, connectivity . . .

Historically, large organizations have sought to embed and extend that phase of their life-cycle which provides the most stable and durable profits, leveraging their dominance to curtail change and deter new market entrants. That's understandable, but the problem—especially as markets become more dynamic—is that a reluctance to innovate becomes a long-term vulnerability when the barriers to entry fall. The recent rise of app-based or digital banks offering simpler and unstuffy services to younger consumers, are a typical example of how the retail banking industry was caught short—and is now racing to catch up.

Hence encouraging innovation, even in stable times, is critical to avoiding complacency and, to my mind, one of the most essential values and behaviors for an organization to embrace. It's often said that new entrants don't require the same returns or have the same shareholder expectations as established players. That may be true, but innovation is, at least in relative terms, much more costly and existentially risky for those start-ups. For established players to be paralyzed by the desire to protect their maximal profit point is both ironic and a dereliction of their longer-term duties to shareholders.

Leaders must step up here, making the case for sustainability through change and allowing space for their organizational mavericks and shamans. By definition, these will be few, and indeed it can be harmful to have too many at the top table, but listening and, more importantly, paying attention to more radical perspectives are critical to staying ahead of the disruption curve.

So too is staying agile. Innovation seldom proceeds in giant leaps or eureka-like epiphanies. Most times it requires adaptive thinking, which might mean going one way today and another tomorrow. The role of leaders is to create the mindset that drives this forward, showing a willingness to alter direction in the face of new evidence. Humility, listening, and, most of all, a meritocratic culture in which the best ideas win, are among the foundations of the constructive disruption that leaders have a responsibility to foster.

As with so many of today's leadership challenges, I believe the most effective response to the threats and opportunities we face lies in the values our organizations live by. A vision and reward system that's based on stasis will neither inspire nor sustain—and it will not attract the talent that rightly expects greater trust in the devolved expertise of the organization. One of the hardest judgment calls for all leaders is to know when to cede their expertise and authority to others. When faced with market disruption, it is never truer that the skills and qualities which got us to where we are will not be sufficient for where we need to go.

I don't want to imply that the solutions are straightforward. The reason for the hard toll of business failures is not only that market leaders have the most to lose. It's also because strategic alternatives require imagination, courage, and the support of all stakeholders in what is inevitably a less than certain outcome. What's clear, however, is that a failure to embrace evolving realities, even when those threats may not appear urgent, will ultimately lead to a greater and more harmful disconnect. In the future, we must break with the expectation that equates stability with value, and instead accept that disruption is now part of business as usual.

ANALYSIS AND CREATIVITY—FELLOWS OR FOES?

PRESIDENT RONALD REAGAN, SPEAKING after talks with Soviet leader Mikhail Gorbachev at the Reykjavik summit in 1986, infamously said that what was most needed between the superpowers was *trust* ... adding, after a dramatic pause, ... *but verify!* The apparent contradiction made headlines around the world, helping to foster an approach that led to the Strategic Arms Reduction Treaty and the removal of around 80 percent of the nuclear warheads in existence.

This phrase is actually not Reagan's at all, but an old Russian proverb which serves to illustrate that a counterintuitive tension is often the most effective way to break down those barriers that impede step change progress. Its wisdom is now commonplace, aided by the growth of technology that gives confidence to more progressive attitudes: "trust trading," for example, is standard practice among retail partners; customs checks are made on random samples; we trust our people but verify their output ...

All of which is intended as a prompt to reflect on how we might apply similar thinking to our organizations. What, as business leaders, can we do to foster the relationships and environment that supports the creative progress we need? And how do we balance the need for innovation, with the equally necessary reassurance that our actions are founded on more than a leap of faith?

Fresh thinking is essential to progress. Without it, we stagnate, our horizons narrow, and our competitors overtake us. At a macro level, the impetus for change is essential for human flourishing—it's no coincidence that when innovation dries up, or is curtailed by dogma, we talk of "Dark Ages" or "closed societies." History is littered with examples of the damage this causes, just as it also confirms the benefits of freethinking and the open society.

We all know this, and yet the reality is that when it comes to our own circumstances, creative leaps can be scary and uncertain, evoking what the historian Robert Hughes brilliantly described as "the shock of the new." His interest lay in the arts, but the same sequence of "disruption, resistance, and progress" is seen in the scientific and industrial revolutions that preceded our modern era. And today, the pattern continues, most obviously in the digital sphere, which has supercharged the speed and reach—but also the risks—of creative innovation.

It is a mistake, however, to think of creativity purely in terms of inspirational genius. As James Dyson, the billionaire UK engineer and inventor, has pointed out—practical progress is seldom made in the manner of Archimedes in his bath or Isaac Newton under the apple tree. Rather, it's an iterative journey, which sharpens our notions and intuition through a process of trial, error, and adjustment. Dyson has filed over 4,000 patents and yet he claims none of his ideas were truly unique—what made the difference is his commitment to the hard hours of testing and adjustment that irons out the flaws and solves problems in a piecemeal way.

Dyson also argues that innovation flourishes most in an atmosphere of creative tension, where ideas are robustly and competitively challenged, often in partnerships or teams, in pursuit of a common goal. We see this pattern time and again in art and science: Picasso and

Braque, Darwin and Wallace, Lennon and McCartney... The relevance for business leaders is that innovation works best when it's integral to, and not isolated from, the day-to-day realities of the organization. Indeed, research has shown that transformation and development teams work most effectively—and come up with the most productive ideas—when subject to the same rigorous critique and analysis as our everyday processes.

Ground breaking creativity is also a rare event—were it not, then change would simply overwhelm us. The reality is that most great ideas take the form of an inspirational leap which is then refined through marginal gains that make the bigger difference. As an apt illustration, when Dick Fosbury revolutionized the high jump at the 1968 Mexico Olympics, he won by a mere 2cm, clearing 2.24m for gold—today, after universal adoption of and, critically, refinement to his groundbreaking technique—the world record stands at 2.45m.

These sorts of gains come not from pondering on the stars, but from analyzing what works best, finding ways to improve on the idea, and being open to our failures. The writer Matthew Syed, explores this idea in his deeply persuasive and accessible book, *Black Box Thinking*. Syed cites the aviation industry as the ultimate example of progressively learning from both failure and innovation—its embrace of objective analysis taking air travel from what was once the riskiest, to what is currently the safest, form of mass transportation.

Analysis is therefore the bedfellow, and not the bugaboo, of practical creativity. For by measuring and learning, not only do we sort the wheat from the chaff, we also help the good become great—or more often, just that little bit better. Malcolm Gladwell has a wonderful podcast which explores this process through the evolution of Leonard Cohen's song, "Hallelujah". The piece took years to gestate, slowly improving its form and lyrics to become one of the most recognized classics in modern songwriting.

The operative phrase in the paragraph above is "little bit better." That's something different to reinvention, and yet ironically it requires a similar mindset. Though on reflection, maybe it's not ironic at all—for now I think about it, the most analytic people I've worked with are among the best innovators —and almost all creatives I know are deeply analytic in their approach.

Which brings me back to my opening example. For Ronald Reagan to make the breakthrough with Russia, he needed a creative leap of the type scientist Edward de Bono described when he wrote about shifting perspectives by throwing off old patterns. But to make it work—for the gains to truly stick—he needed something more; something that the great American poet, Henry Wadsworth Longfellow, might have taught him— "The heights by great men reached and kept were not attained by sudden flight, but they, while their companions slept, were toiling upward in the night."

THE MORAL MAZE OF DECISION MAKING

AS I SIT DOWN to write this article in the solitude of my study, there are people gathering in churches across the United States, encouraged by their preachers to come together for worship. In a secular equivalent, the politically faithful are being urged to attend party rallies over the coming weeks. And all of this in the midst of a Coronavirus pandemic where the clear scientific advice is that public assemblies will lead to the seeding of infection and a significantly greater loss of life.

It's not my purpose to criticize the actions of those who chose to attend their churches or hustings. These people are not foolish, nor can we assume they are indifferent to the suffering of others. My tendency to put caution over civil liberties is a personal view, and the public mood is seldom characterized by universal agreement even if a sober consideration of the facts were possible. When the issues have become politicized, as is certainly true in this case, it's inevitable that we'll see passion on either side.

But despite these caveats, I'm still left pondering—and troubled by—the stark conflict between the near universal advice of independent experts on the one hand and the actions of those influencers who have an interest in a different outcome, on the other. Perhaps my discomfort is rooted in the notion that this friction is not unique to politics or pandemics. In some form or other, ethical trade-offs are inherent to most businesses of some scale and the value judgments we make in resolving them are a signature to our leadership.

The behavior of the tobacco industry is a case study in the moral pressures within corporations. Over many decades, the leading firms marketed their products as safe and socially desirable, despite clear evidence that smoking was both highly addictive and a direct contributor to premature deaths. A culture of denial fostered a resistance to health warnings, restrictions on advertising, or any other measures which might discourage sales. In what has become an archetypal example of ethics vs. economics, the historic practices of the tobacco industry have been rightly condemned.

While this is one of the clearest of cases, there are countless others where the ethical considerations are less obvious and prominent in the public consciousness. In the sphere of logistics, for example, how do we best balance obligations to shareholders with a responsibility for the environment? Should vehicle manufacturers have a duty to lead on low emissions, or is it reasonable for them to wait for legislation which creates a level playing field? And what of biodegradable packaging, or fair-trade sourcing, or raising wages above a strictly competitive threshold? When first movers bear the burden of risk, is it ethical to hold back from the morally principled but commercially disadvantageous course?

There are some who would seek to deny the existence of the conflict, arguing that an appraisal of long-term costs and benefits will show the right path forward, leading to the appropriate balance in the medium— or long—term. Perhaps so, but it's significant that few of those taking this stance are at the sharp end of business. It's easy to promote an ethical utopia when all is academic and removed—if you're the third placed player in a market, pressured on all sides by competition and expectations, try convincing your investors or employees that you should be at the bleeding edge of ethical change.

Even a lesser goal of *playing our part* or *doing the right thing* assumes that the moral course is relatively clear and divisible. In practice, we live in an interconnected world, where our actions—no matter how well meaning—can have a butterfly effect that is beyond prediction. We should be skeptical of supposed solutions that take insufficient account of their own uncertainty. For all of the urgency of those passionate for change (the activist environmental movement is a good example here), history has shown that the messy process of evolution is usually a surer—and safer—route to success than five-year plans or Arcadian visions of a great leap forward.

And what about the multiple instances in which we are faced with a choice between competing virtues? My opening example is ultimately a tension between the civil liberties we have come to expect and a desire to protect the health of the wider population. Article 11 of the Human Rights Act, 1998, seeks to guarantee a freedom of assembly and association but caveats this with proportionate restrictions that protect the health and freedoms of other people. The critical word in that clause is 'proportionate' but unfortunately there is no strict definition we can turn to.

So how, as organizational leaders, do we navigate this moral minefield?

I'd propose that for most of us, the way through is not to become philosophers but to pursue a course of what I call *principled pragmatism*. As that label suggests, we should focus more on the optimum than the perfect. It's close to what Aristotle would call the Golden Mean—a path between deficiency and excess, underpinned by good intentions and a care for others.

And more tangibly, I'd offer five maxims that we could all adopt regardless of circumstance.

Be agnostic. When considering the thorniest of issues, I find it helpful to ask 'what course would I chose if I didn't yet know how it impacted me?' Would I, for example, introduce universal healthcare care if my immediate or future requirement for health care was not revealed until after I'd made the choice? How would I structure the executive bonus if I didn't know what position I had in the firm—or if I were an employee or a customer? When ignorant of our personal best interest, the most rational course is to choose the fairest for all.

Focus on direction not destination. Most progress is a journey, not an event. Indeed, my belief that markets and their morals evolve means there's never an end point we can reach. It's therefore vital that we consider the course and the speed at which we're traveling, rather than being obsessed with our arrival.

Don't be dogmatic. Many ethical judgments, and the evidence supporting them, are not as clear cut as leaders would wish. As with parenting, playing soccer or, for that matter mastering an instrument—all of us make mistakes. The important thing is that we correct them, responding to feedback and facts rather than digging in our heels.

Beware of moral myopia. Publicly prominent concerns can often feel compelling, and at times it's vital that we react to these with speed and clarity. The recent Black Lives Matter campaign is a good example of how long-overdue progress can follow from a sea change in sentiment. But we should be wary of being too short-sighted—it's better to set a course, and truly steer it, than to react to every twist and turn of public opinion.

Communicate the trade-offs. If you need to make compromises, then be clear on what they are and why you're making them. Explain the mitigation for any negative consequences and how these might lessen over time. This helps everyone understand that doing the right thing is seldom a binary choice.

Returning to those gatherings that are happening as I write: I must be one of the few people who has spent time throughout this crisis in the US, the UK, and mainland Europe. The divergences I've experienced in the public's attitude and mood are striking. In part they reflect cultural characteristics, but I'd suggest that trust in our politicians and advisors is the critical difference. And it seems to me that to win that confidence, leaders of all types must first and foremost show that while the world and the choices we face are invariably imperfect, at least our intentions are good.

AUTHOR'S NOTE:

THE FOLLOWING TWO ARTICLES were written when I was CEO of a UK listed PLC in need of significant transformation; my intended audience was as much internal colleagues as any wider public. In republishing them here I was first inclined to revise and broaden their scope, but before doing so I paused to consider whether there was greater relevance and integrity in their original form.

Reading them again, there is nothing I disagree with today; their message, and the values on which they are founded, continue to sit comfortably with my belief that nurturing talent is vital to sustainable progress. The articles show too how challenge and reflection can broaden our opinions, with value being added from outside perspectives.

If there is one aspect which in hindsight I would wish to have expanded on, it is the need for greater diversity in our organizations and society as whole. Research supports what recent events—both globally and domestically— have confirmed: that we are stronger when we embrace and incorporate a wider range of views, and weaker the more we insist on a monocultural perception of what constitutes relevant contributions.

To sustainably prosper today, we must actively seek a full range of contributions, be they founded on skill, experience, race, gender, age, sexuality, faith, and many more qualities I could list. This is not to suggest that the talent strategies of companies should be managed in accordance with some abstract demographic algorithm—nor that should we pursue diversity to the point at which it risks diluting our expertise and focus. But it is to assert that in an interconnected and interdependent world, it's no longer credible or indeed desirable to define talent and what constitutes valuable contribution as narrowly as has historically been the case.

And so, with the caveat that our perspectives—including those opinions expressed here—need always to broaden and be open to reflection, I am happy to publish the articles unchanged (other than minor corrections for US spelling and grammar).

NURTURING TALENT AND NAVIGATING THE ROAD TO SUCCESS

A FEW WEEKS AGO, I gave an interview in which I reflected on the importance of building talent across companies, the need for structures that facilitate career progression, and most of all, a supportive culture which allows talent to thrive by learning from our mistakes as well as our successes. There are compelling reasons, I said, for investing in talent, and on that point, I guess few business leaders would disagree. But as with many organizational challenges, while the way ahead might be obvious, sticking to the path isn't always so straight forward.

Let's start with some guiding principles.

Talent is vital to making good decisions. With talented people, and talented teams, we not only perform better today, but we enhance our strategic vision and tactical planning. The short-term advantage and the sustainability of that success go hand in hand. Look at any successful sports team and you'll see their stars are on the field—with the occasional genius amongst them—but always on the bench are the next generation, pushing for places, eager to learn, encouraged by their mentors.

Talent thrives best in open and supportive cultures. For colleagues to flourish, they need to know that in taking the next step they'll receive support, some space for learning, and the confidence to know they can be themselves. That last point is important—because true talent management isn't about the rote learning of skills and procedures; it's about nurturing a diversity of unique and valuable contributions to the overall goal.

And lastly, talent is a responsibility we all share. Sure, the People Teams often take a lead in coordinating training and development programs and the like—and rightly so. But for talent to truly thrive, we need leaders at all levels to see that bringing on the next generation is part of what makes for a sustainably better business. Finding opportunities to give some trust, providing tools and resources, as well as spotting the talent gaps—and occasional blockages—are just as vital a skill for managers as hitting their sales or cost targets.

But if that much is straightforward—what is it that gets in the way?

Fear of failure is perhaps the biggest constraint, especially if it leads to us avoiding risks. For without some unpredictability—to ourselves as well as the organization—progress isn't possible. Effective leaders learn from mistakes and making them is a key part of a continuous improvement ethos. So, we need a culture that empowers us to make decisions and an environment that helps enhance the quality of the choices we make. Inclusive, interactive teams help to grow talent by sharing perspectives and considering possibilities—in so doing, while individuals can thrive, the outcomes can be shared by others too. Putting it another way, constructive risk taking isn't about jumping blindly off cliffs—it's about weighing up the options and then acting with focus and commitment.

Resistance to change is an obstacle too. Indeed, it is often the biggest blocker to talent, and one of the most cited reasons why ambitious people leave otherwise good organizations. If ideas and ingenuity are stymied, then stagnation and attrition surely follow—and guess what, talented people can smell it a mile off! The result is a drain on knowledge and a creativity void that ends in a vicious circle of yet more fear and failure. Like with risk, embracing change doesn't mean an unquestioning drive to revolution; positive change blends evolution with bold decisions that move us forward at pace. By working this way, we nurture talent in tandem with the opportunities we pursue.

And lastly, we need clear measures of success. For without these, it's all too easy to misrepresent progress or excuse the lack of it. Of course, nurturing talent isn't as objective as math, but neither is it some enigmatic quality that resists common sense assessment. That's why we need talent driven KPIs throughout the organization, working to agreed outcomes and focusing resolutely on their achievement.

So how best do we navigate our way to success?

In my organization today, we have core values that keep us on track. We're creating a culture of diversity and inclusion, where colleagues can be themselves at work, and the opportunity to develop their careers is encouraged and celebrated. Our values of trust, fairness, creativity, and openness are a compass, guiding our decisions to ensure we make the most of our individual and collective potential.

And we're backing this up with investment in training and communications, despite a pressure for savings in tough markets. For me, this is part of our duty as leaders; we have a responsibility to all our stakeholders—be they colleagues, customers, shareholders, or lenders —to ensure the organization is fit for the future, and that's not something we can put on hold. Nurturing talent is fundamental to building a sustainable and constantly improving business, and if at times it feels like a complex jigsaw, we should remember that it's when the parts come together that the bigger picture emerges.

As the first measure of our progress, I expect to see succession routes for all key roles, with training plans for our high potential colleagues and a map of the talent gaps we need to fill. Alongside this should be a more empowered culture with broad levels of authority, sharing success but also learning from its mistakes through post-mortem analysis based on a zero-blame approach. In truth, there are many more indicators we should expect: cross functional working, creative thinking, reduced duplication . . . I could go on.

But isn't it also true that genuine progress needs to be widespread and self-evident? Just as we can all recognize talent in sport or science or the arts, so too we instinctively know when it's present in the workplace. The ultimate goal is therefore that nurturing talent becomes part of our DNA, a virtue we pass from one generation to another, with care for its continuity, and a sense of creating something bigger than ourselves.

BUILDING—AND BLENDING—TALENT FOR THE FUTURE

LAST AUTUMN I GAVE an interview and later wrote about the importance of developing talent in organizations. My claim was that by creating opportunities for people to grow, we reap the reward of their unique and valuable contributions to our overall goal. That much, I said, is mainstream progressive thinking—so much so, that my substantive point was that sticking to the path isn't always as easy as it seems. Certainly, I'd not expected the core view to be challenged.

However, some weeks ago a former colleague put it to me that investing in talent wasn't enough; what's more, she pointed out, there were numerous examples where I'd personally hired senior leaders in a way that had potentially leapfrogged others in the organization. Surely, she suggested, there were times when building from within is too slow or too haphazard for the needs of a particular situation.

And, of course, like all fair challenges, she was right—at least in part.

A commitment to growing and giving space to talent remains fundamental to the health of most companies. It's especially appropriate in working towards long-term goals, when the workforce is relatively stable and, importantly, when there's sufficient scale and opportunity to allow for regular career progression. Absent some or all of these conditions and the strategy is clearly less productive. But even in the most vibrant and forward-thinking of organizations, there will still be occasions when an injection from outside can be both necessary and beneficial.

The impetus from fresh perspectives, particularly during periods of change, should not be underestimated. Nor too should the objectivity which external recruits can bring, helping to counterbalance the established cultures and processes which constrain all of our abilities to see things differently. And sometimes, particularly in markets that are changing rapidly, there's a critical need for skills and insights that simply can't be developed in-house. Recruitment for these purposes comes at a cost, but if done wisely I believe there's no inherent conflict with a wider commitment to internal talent and succession plan.

Similarly, there are times when organizations require a short-term injection of skills that would be uneconomic or suboptimal to develop internally. Technology projects, for example, often need experts in coding and system architecture, just as transformation programs will benefit from change management specialists. Even those companies with a depth of internal skills to draw on are likely to have specialist partners to help with areas such as branding, legal matters, or senior recruitment.

This blended approach to internal and external talent is the reality, if not the stated strategy, of most sizeable companies. It's sometimes referred to as the "build-buy-borrow" approach, and the skill is to get the balance right over time while meeting the needs of each situation. Too much emphasis on external recruitment, for example, will lead to demotivation and insufficient embedded knowledge; similarly, outsourcing works best when delivered through trusted partners who understand not only the immediate goals but also the culture and values of the organization, and often its history too.

As an aside, one of the differences I've observed over recent years is the extent to which temporary appointments are significantly more common in the UK than the US. Indeed, in the UK, it's now not unusual to come across interim specialists whose career is founded on a mix of troubleshooting, project management, and "minding the shop" before the arrival of a permanent appointment. At their best, these specialists can be skilled at driving through the quick and sometimes difficult decisions that a crisis or void demands—but a soon as we turn to look at the longer term, the attractions of interim appointments strike me as limited. As a former colleague once put it to me: *interims are a very sharp tool—to be used for precision and with appropriate care.*

Returning to the original theme, while I've counter-argued that a blended approach to recruitment is compatible with a commitment to talent, there's much truth in the suggestion that investment alone is not enough. Even a casual interest in the history of sports will show that the building of great teams is never just about money. Similarly, pouring cash into training and development programs, without the appropriate culture and opportunity to support the aspirations this fosters, will lead only to roadblocks and frustration; at worst, you'll end up training colleagues on behalf of your competitors, which is where they're likely to head.

Two weeks ago, the UK's *Sunday Times* published the latest results of its annual "Best Companies to Work For" survey. The poll is a long-established benchmark of employee engagement as measured by colleague opinions—to score highly, it's not enough to have good policies on paper, they must truly resonate with employees across a range of workplace measures. As the "Best Companies" website neatly summarizes, at these leading companies *". . . employees encounter inspirational leaders, charitable and environmental initiatives built into work life, a focus on staff wellbeing, fair financial rewards, skills-boosting training and career progression, excellent managers, and teammates who inspire both admiration and fun."*

That's quite a list—and in scanning the results, it struck me that the majority of the businesses which ranked highly, were not necessarily the household names we might expect. This suggests it's not simply the aura of a brand or even scale which makes colleagues feel they have opportunity, rather, their satisfaction is primarily sustained by an ambition to succeed together, underpinned by values that respect them as individuals.

So, what of the concerns raised by my former colleague? It's certainly true that there have been occasions when I've hired in external talent, and in most (though not all) cases, I'd do so again. And I agree that a sole focus on in-house skills, no matter how well resourced, is unlikely to be sufficient. Indeed, given the uncertainties of commerce and the pace at which change occurs, I doubt any of the leading companies in the *Sunday Times* survey follow a single-track strategy. But for all that, a blended approach is a more accurate description of what most businesses will follow, without an underlying commitment to progress through people their options are likely to be more limited, and less sustainable.

In many ways, I was pleased to receive the challenge. I enjoyed the discussion, and in truth, our positions were inches apart. Importantly, it was offered in a constructive spirit, as an opportunity to explore and learn together. And I'd argue that's exactly the approach we most need to nurture: a desire to find the best way forward, founded on a commitment to each and all of our abilities, offering scope for personal growth, while welcoming newcomers and the skills and perspectives they bring.

SHAPING

OUR PATHS ARE SHAPED BY A SERIES OF
DECISIONS, MISTAKES AND DEFINING
MOMENTS - THERE IS NO STRAIGHT LINE
TO THE OUR TRUTH.

You are not here merely to make a living, you are here in order to enable the world to live more amply, with greater vision, with a finer spirit of hope and achievement. You are here to enrich the world, and you impoverish yourself if you forget the errand.

Woodrow Wilson

TWENTY-TWENTY VISION

HAS IT REALLY BEEN twenty years since we were celebrating a new Millennium? Depending on your perspective, that milestone might seem like yesterday or an age away—given the pace of change, it can feel like both. Across societies worldwide, there's a cultural tradition of acknowledging significant anniversaries and using these as a time to reflect on the past and set new goals. And so, as we enter the third decade of the century, it's perhaps an appropriate moment to consider the road we've travelled and the forces and challenges that are likely to lie ahead.

From a leadership perspective, looking back on the last twenty years, the landscape is in many respects still recognizable—the basics of balanced analytical judgment, good people skills, team building and empowerment, are little different, if more nuanced. But the changes wrought by technology, increasing globalization, public sentiment, and the sheer improvements to our understanding of how we best work together, have inexorably transformed the way organizations navigate their routes to success.

My chief interest lies in the impact these developments—and many others—will have on the demands of senior leadership in the decade ahead. Of course, cultural trends don't fit neatly into ten-year cycles, but for the sake of convenience—and with a heavy caveat that *futurology* is out of date the moment it's voiced—these are my thoughts on some of the issues that may most significantly impact the leadership agenda over the next ten years.

PURPOSE

The idea of organizational purpose has been gaining ground for some time. It's understood that businesses must make a profit to survive, but beyond this there lies an increasingly powerful sentiment that organizations need to play a clearer and more positive role, not only for their direct stakeholders but also in wider society. The growing B Corp movement, which accredits businesses on social and environmental factors, has to date been seen as somewhat *alternative*, but its core message, which envisions business as a force for good while campaigning for a more balanced assessment of positive impacts than profit alone, is increasingly influencing mainstream thinking. Evidence shows that organizations founded on strong social values have more engaged colleagues, attract talent at less cost, and enjoy stronger customer relations and brand reputations. Leadership in the next decade will require greater attention to these issues, not as a requisite of political correctness, but as a means to drive performance.

SUSTAINABILITY

No organization of size can ignore sustainability in the coming decade. From an environmental perspective, the pressures are literally rapidly warming up—and with them a need for greater vision and bolder solutions. Pressure groups demanding targets that would appear, by conventional standards, to be unachievable and unrealistic, are nonetheless impacting public sentiment and, with that, shaping policy and legislative agendas. The challenge for many leaders will be that adopting a 'road to Damascus' eco-conversion will be as impractical as continuing to ignore the underlying realities. My expectation is that a combination of technological solutions and ever more stringent legislation (particularly to ensure level playing fields) will help, but regardless of the detail, it is clear that we will require leaders to step up with urgency and place these issues at the center of our planning.

TRANSPARENCY

The last two decades have seen an unprecedented increase in the scope of corporate reporting. Financial performance, though remaining preeminent, is now only one among many of the measures that organizations must account for: gender diversity, pay ratios, executive incentives, environmental emissions, health and safety. This wider assessment of organizational competence will only increase, as will the transparency of data comparison between organizations.

My sense is that we will see the pendulum swing the other way, with a greater demand for leaders to provide more detailed narratives that are answerable to (and tested by) the ever-increasing transparency of the data. Accountability and transparency go hand in hand, so we should expect leaders to be more answerable to their stakeholders than ever before.

COLLECTIVITY

One thing that isn't going to happen is life becoming simpler. Complexity will necessarily increase as a consequence of the challenges above, and it's as true as ever that *what got us to here, will not take us to where we need to go.* In this environment, leadership that's focused on a single individual, however charismatic or talented, will not be sufficient—and even a united senior team is unlikely to deliver the transformational change that some organizations will require. The most successful companies already devolve decision making, but simply segmenting responsibility (by, for example, allocating values to HR or efficiencies to operations) will also not be enough. As complexity increases, the role of leadership must shift even further from a focus on decision making and control, to that of engendering a collective ownership of direction and priorities. In short, leadership will increasingly be about demonstrably living the organization's collective values and goals as much as setting them.

COURAGE

The average lifespan of a business is shortening—it's currently somewhere around ten years—and most of those long-standing companies that continue to thrive do so by continual adaptation if not entire reinvention. We all know that the last decade has hit the retail sector particularly hard but arguably greater and more fundamental challenges lie ahead for others—consider the challenges facing the leaders in say, heavy engineering, hi-tech manufacturing, distribution, combustible engine manufacturing.

For many businesses—be they start-ups or global giants—the next decade is likely to involve some truly critical calls. Leaders will need to listen, to delegate, to set goals—all that we have considered so far—but they must also have courage, since many of the key decisions will require acting on beliefs in the absence of certainty. The word *courage* has its origins in the old French and Latin words for *heart* or *seat of our feelings*—and in that sense, it is subtly different to bravery or resolve. These qualities will be helpful too, for boldness and determination are how we must put our beliefs into practice, and acting together, they will be as fundamental to success as any analysis or epiphany.

ZEST

I was tempted to title this last section "fun," for enjoyment of the task is surely essential in any leader, whatever their era. But in *zest* I am hinting at something more. For if we bring energy and enthusiasm to the mix—ideally in a manner that's infectious to others—then what's daunting becomes exciting; what seems an obstacle becomes an opportunity—and thereby all the more achievable.

Leaders must not fear the challenges of the next ten years—rather, they should see them as a golden chance: unique, inspiring, and seminal to our futures. Leadership in this context is a privilege. Remembering as much, each time we turn up for our colleagues or ourselves, leadership will be a challenge we constantly forward too.

Happy New Year—and here's to a Roaring Twenties!

THE POWER OF CLAPPING

AT 8.00 PM ON Thursday 26 March, the citizens of the United Kingdom stood at their doorsteps and balconies to applaud the doctors, nurses, and caretakers of the National Health Service. As the nation steeled itself for the peak of the Covid-19 crisis, millions took a moment to express their gratitude and assert the message that we are *in this together*. When I joined my neighbors in clapping at the sky, the collective goodwill was tangible.

The gesture was not unique to the UK. Indeed, there had been similar events in the Netherlands and my home country of Belgium. But it is perhaps significant that the health service should be the primary focus here, where the NHS has a unifying force that I'd venture exceeds even other iconic British symbols, such as its much-loved monarchy. The goodwill shown towards the NHS as an institution is stronger than any commercial brand, any political party, and at times, any objective reasoning . . .

In that moment, to comment on the unfolding crisis risked the possibility of gross imprecision, as events continued to develop in ways that we could not foresee. Over a matter of days, the policies of governments across the globe turned on a dime; at times, a sort of "hysteria in small increments," only to arrive at where we should first have started. Thankfully, there is now consensus in Europe, if not the US, that containment of the virus is best achieved by temporary lockdowns of personal movement—and that this is the only acceptable way forward.

But as we go on facing into the privations this involves, it will take more than legislation to see us through. Liberal democracies do not draw their strength from the strict imposition or literal interpretation of emergency laws, however necessary or democratically legitimate they may be. Rather, they thrive on the communal values and unity of purpose that was so effectively demonstrated that Thursday night.

The power of collective sentiment is well known—you need only to look at the stock market to see the impact it can have. Politicians nurture it, brands thrive on it; the "goodwill" on company balance sheets is effectively much the same thing. Over recent years, the use of "nudge theory" has sought to identify small prompts that stimulate positive behavior in areas where legislation would be complex or difficult to police. The charging of a nominal sum for single use shopping bags has become a case study in how to influence good choices, as, on a lighter note, is the painting of a fly on public urinals to improve the aim!

For now, it seems we are at least agreed—and have found a collective goodwill—on the need for containment. The question, therefore, which most interests me, is whether we can also stand together in support of the "exit strategy" that, in time, we will surely need. At present, this may appear of secondary importance, but its relevance to our future should not be underestimated.

Writing in *The Financial Times*, early in the first UK lockdown, the historian and philosopher Yuval Noah Harari claimed the decisions we took in the next few weeks would shape the world for years to come. His prediction is almost certainly correct. At a policy level we will need changes to healthcare, to travel, to emergency procedures; we may all—though I hope with real caution—need to be more accepting of restrictions to our liberty.

But what of the public sentiment which will underlie and legitimize these choices? Will we retreat to the false security of a more closed world, or have faith in a future that's based on greater cooperation and knowledge sharing? Can we muster the altruism and trust to coordinate an economic recovery, or will we emerge from the wreckage in a way that resembles the panic-buying and squabbles we've seen in our supermarkets?

These decisions will be determined not so much by our governments and institutions, as by each and every one of us. For, as the recent policy pirouettes have shown, it is our collective actions and attitudes that will most influence those who act in our name. Across the world, economic rescue packages have been put in place; policies that would have been unthinkable were it not for the public mood that we must stand in unison and shoulder the short-term costs.

As we emerge from the crisis, I wonder if we, as individuals will exhibit the same generosity? Among those thousands who've had flights cancelled, how many of us will accept a credit voucher rather than demanding a refund? When commerce returns and our customers need more time to pay, how swiftly will we, as business leaders, move to foreclose? And as shareholders, can we refrain from punishing those companies that are far-sighted enough to support their partners over the restoration of dividends?

The economic and social exit we achieve will be the accumulation of the answers we give to these—and countless more—specific questions. I hope we can sustain our goodwill—for as with most aspects of life, we will reap what we sow. Our governments can nudge us, our banks can support us (no doubt with gritted teeth) but ultimately, to come through this crisis stronger, we must sustain the collective sentiment that requires no words, but was so clearly heard in our standing and clapping together that week.

NAVIGATING THE
MIDDLE GROUND

FOR THE LAST FEW weeks, we've been bombarded with advice on how to make best use of this period of lockdown. The internet is awash with potted wisdom on how to be more organized, distracted, or upgraded, while my inbox has personalized suggestions ranging from cleaning up the sock drawer to learning a new language or getting that old guitar down from the attic. Meanwhile, events unfold beyond our control in a way that adds to a sense of disempowerment and ennui.

Much the same is true for businesses. Countless articles offer pointers on *planning for a post-Covid future* or *the best online training tools* . . . In the equivalent of the suggestions to tidy our wardrobes, enterprises are urged to catch up on admin or, at the other extreme, prepare strategies to win market share at the expense of their less diligent competitors. For all that the counsel may be well-meaning, it generally misses the mark.

The reason for this will be obvious to anyone who juggles the daily demands of business or for that matter, family life. While nobody suggests it's not a virtue to clear our emails or catch up on personal development, the reality is that most organizations get by perfectly well with a long to-do list. And as for developing radical new strategies, it's a brave, arguably foolhardy, enterprise that places any serious bets on a future that's beyond its knowing.

As human beings, we experience the world, and perform at our best, when navigating the middle ground. You may—like me—be captivated by those popular science documentaries on astronomy or quantum physics, but for all of us, the extremes of time and space are still impossible to fully comprehend. What's more, even if we could, the knowledge would make little difference to our everyday lives—that we are hurtling through space at a million miles an hour won't save you from a speeding fine, and if you jump that red light, good luck in arguing that color is only a matter of perception!

Something similar is equally true of commerce. The day-to-day reality is that success comes less from having perfectly granular policies or all-embracing strategies, than it does from the thousands of judgments that are the warp and weft of our trading relationships. It's this daily grind—and the grit in the oyster that comes with it—that we understand best; it's actually what motivates us, what enables us to feel empowered, and what most allows us to shine.

Our need then, in exiting this crisis, will overwhelmingly be for pragmatism rather than principle, and certainly not dogma. This doesn't mean we should abandon all structures or strategic vision, but it does suggest we should focus our minds on the underlying purpose of the choices we will need to make. In this sense, the return to a *new normal* will require a commercial equivalent of the "practical reasoning" that's advocated by thinkers such as Peter Singer or the late Mary Midgely. Malcom Gladwell's recent podcasts on the pliability of Jesuit thinking—and its resolution of issues in the context of the world as we actually live it—are instructive guides too.

In re-establishing our trading partnerships, the call to exercise discretion will be greater than ever—be it cash flow, refunds, sales targets, or staff bonuses, pragmatic solutions and reciprocal understanding will be the currency of success. *Black Swan events—a* term coined by Nassim Nicholas Taleb for major, unforeseen situations we are unprepared for—invariably leave us with a world that's changed beyond previous experience. But this pandemic is not an extinction event, and it is only by working through the aftershock—instance by instance, customer by customer—that we will find and shape the opportunities that determine our future.

The reason the current lockdown is so difficult for many of us—and for our organizations—to bear, is that despite all the well-meaning advice—and no matter how tidy our socks or ambitious our visions—it's only when this quarantine is lifted that we can be truly productive again. The people and the enterprises which succeed will not be those with empty inboxes or even the best laid plans—they will be those who make the smartest calls in the mucky middle ground of decision making that is the stuff of business as we know it.

LEADERSHIP AND OUR MOST POWERFUL TOOL IN A TIME CRISIS

THE CORONAVIRUS PANDEMIC IS a crisis in the form we haven't seen for generations—not only because of the scale of mortality (which is unbearably tragic, yet hopefully less than many military conflicts) but because of its global nature, its stealthy attributes, our wretched ability to control its spread, and perhaps most of all, the rude awakening that there are limits to the power of human ingenuity in the face of unrestrained nature.

For all our scientific progress, the justified response of the developed world has essentially been little different to medieval times—isolate, wash your hands, and be wary of strangers. Making matters worse, the entangled nature of modern society means these tactics are harder to achieve than in centuries past. But if there is any light in this dark hour, it is surely in our vastly greater potential to communicate and marshal our actions in a coordinated and steadfast manner. In this respect, leadership is arguably our most powerful tool in tackling the tasks that lie ahead.

A crisis is defined as a moment of intense difficulty or danger; a situation when critical decisions must be made. Specifically, it is a time of turning points—when the actions we chose will steer us to either recovery or disaster. Leadership in these circumstances requires more than bravado or gesture politics—it needs a cool head, an ability to take others with us and a clarity of purpose as well as strength and consistency of will.

The internet—especially social media—is currently awash with advice, often with a heavy emphasis on historical examples. To use Nassim Nicholas Taleb's phrase, the Coronavirus is a *Black Swan event* —if we look at the specifics of our situation, there are precious few parallels to draw on.

But if direct lessons from the past are not especially helpful, the principles of good leadership surely still apply: a willingness to listen and learn, a focus on the common good and clarity—and consistency—to our messaging. All of us recognize these qualities, because in the current circumstances we are looking for them in our politicians and influencers—just as we can sense the division that's sown by some of the more closed, partisan, and vastly incoherent responses we've witnessed.

The challenge for leaders is that in this moment of greatest uncertainty, the need to set aside political considerations, to apply measures that have proven to be successful elsewhere, and to provide clarity of purpose and direction is more essential than ever. The philosopher Bertrand Russell wrote that in such circumstances—when the facts and outcomes are at their most opaque—we must focus on the best evidence and reasoning we have, however imperfect it may be. And critically, we must then be resolute until, and unless, new evidence suggests otherwise.

Russell was talking more of intellectual ideas than of crisis management, but his point is still relevant. Leadership, almost by definition, will never please all parties, nor is it intended to. There will always be differences of opinion as to the route we could take—and these should be considered carefully—but there comes a point when a path must be chosen. A leader is someone who forges rather than seeks consensus as Martin Luther King Jr. is attributed with noting.

And ideally, that consensus should help to shape our actions beyond the immediate hiatus. For in returning to the definition of a *Black Swan event*, our world will necessarily be different once the crisis has passed. Think of the various responses to the dissolution of the Soviet Union, and how the decisions which followed have impacted those countries. The contrast between the outcome of the bold action taken by Germany in uniting its country is in stark contrast to the grim realities of many former Soviet states.

In drawing lessons from the past—albeit tangential in their nature—it is relevant that Germany acted with speed as well as clarity of vision. And in returning to the present, it is surely significant that those countries with direct experience of containing the SARS virus have taken some of the strictest and most immediate of measures, proactively focusing on containment and slowing the spread. In contrast, contemplate the graphs of infection levels and mortality peaks in those countries where it quickly became too late to follow their lead.

While I regret that many of us are still in stark denial about the severity of what we have experienced and what may still lie ahead, nonetheless, we will get through this crisis and, in time, assess its consequences with the benefit of hindsight. Ultimately, I suspect and hope we will judge our leaders by their results more than their rhetoric. Meanwhile it's vital that we, all of us, hold onto something less tangible but no less vital for what's to come—and that is, *hope*. For it is our collective belief in a brighter future that most drives and sustains all of human progress. And, at this perilous time, that is perhaps the most powerful tool of all.

LIGHT ON THE HORIZON

ON 8 DECEMBER 2020 in the city of Coventry in the UK, Margaret Kennan received the first publicly administered dose of the Pfizer/ BioNTech vaccine. At ninety-one years old, she described the experience as "the best early birthday present," reflecting worldwide joy that, just possibly, this marked the beginning of the end of the COVID-19 pandemic. As I write, three weeks later, millions across the globe have been inoculated, markets have rebounded and we approach the New Year with rays of light that were well below the horizon only a few months ago.

And yet, dark clouds remain. Because, for all that the vaccine— and equivalent treatments from other biotech companies—represents a triumph of science, before the first shot was administered there were protestations from some quarters. Fueled by social media, conspiracy theorists played on the fears of an already nervous population, peddling claims at times so ludicrous that they beggar belief. In what is almost the ultimate case of *repeat your message regardless,* they've succeeded in spooking a small but not insubstantial section of the public into questioning whether they might skip the treatment just when it's needed most.

There are multiple issues at play here, and not the time or space to deal with them all. I'm going to consign claims that the vaccine will track us via 5G communication or harbors secretly implanted microchips to the dustbin of implausibility in which they belong. Whether we should allow airtime to such theories strikes me as a fine balance between freedom of expression versus the potential for public harm. Time will no doubt expose the nonsense, but sadly it seems there will always be some who choose to disregard the common-sense reasoning by which they lead their daily lives.

More concerning than the unhinged conspirators, are the mumblings that the vaccines are medically unsafe, that they've been developed too quickly, and the safest route is to pass on the treatment. What we have here is the consequence of a not unreasonable first question (*can a vaccine be developed in under a year?*) combining with a mistrust of our political leaders and a misunderstanding of science, to produce a spiral of doubt that risks undermining the whole enterprise.

Or putting the whole thing more bluntly, we have a highly vocal section of society that wants the pandemic to end, but prefers to hang back in the line, leaving the putative *risk* to others.

This is classic *freeriding*, a term usually reserved for scholars, but which most of us know as *not pulling your weight*. In academic terms, freeriding occurs when a party makes no contribution to an enterprise but reaps the same benefits as those whose labor and sacrifice made it possible. Economists regard this as a market failure; philosophers consider it a moral one. To understand why, it's helpful to describe it in more concrete terms.

Imagine you lived in a small pre-industrial agrarian community which needed to irrigate its lands to improve production. All the farmers agree to work together to create a series of ditches and channels, giving two days labor each week in a collective endeavor to deliver a benefit for all. Except, when work begins, one farmer, whose land is in the middle of the project, decides not to take part, focusing instead on building a swanky new house. When the irrigation system is in place, his land benefits and his production increases just the same as the others, and yet, had everyone followed his behavior, the project would not have been possible.

Intuitively we know this is wrong. Which is why John Rawles in his seminal *Theory of Justice* identifies a prohibition on crude freeriding as one of the key principles of a fair society—basing this assertion not just on abstract reasoning, but on focus group after focus group coming to exactly the same conclusion. In the everyday world, it's an economic and social problem that we've developed multiple routes (from taxation to copyright laws) to tackle. But when it comes to medical interventions, we hesitate at compulsion to comply.

And that's understandable because medical procedures raise some especially difficult issues. Questions of free choice and even religious belief come into play—and we are rightly cautious of compelling individuals in what might be seen as personal space. However, it's equally clear that to meaningfully address the biggest social disruption since the second world war, we need the vast majority of us to play our part in the vaccine program. The problem is particularly acute, because those who refuse inoculation increase the risk for others by raising the likelihood that the virus will linger and mutate.

On the whole, western democracies have relied on the personal benefits rather than community obligations to drive a voluntary uptake. As herd immunity builds and our collective risk recedes, we tend to forebear those few who chose to take a different path. Those societies, with a greater emphasis on social cohesion, would take a less tolerant view of their "right" to not comply.

The judgement is a delicate one to make, and not without real and tangible consequences. Only recently, there were outbreaks of measles in the UK that can be directly linked to the now spurious claims about the safety of the MMR vaccine and a consequent reluctance by certain community groups to have their children vaccinated. Many parents who refused cited a belief that they need not worry because of wider herd immunity and that they were concerned about (mis)reported side effects. Their children, who subsequently contracted the disease, are the ones who paid the price of that folly.

Business leaders will face similar issues, for if a company is not a collective endeavor with responsibility to both individuals and wider stakeholders, then what is? What, for example, should be the limits on our expectations of employees? Can we legitimately insist on the vaccination of all colleagues, save perhaps for those with a genuine medical or faith-based reason for exclusion? And what of our customers—in certain sectors (cruise liners, concerts, and sporting events spring to mind) might we insist that proof of vaccination is a pre-requisite of our supplying a service? I suspect, at least in the short term, that some will.

More widely than the recent pandemic, business has an important role to play in nudging behaviors for the communal good. The organizations in which we work are, for many of us, the main place of close interaction with others outside our families. And while we may not use the term *freeriding*, we intuitively know that we have obligations to our colleagues: "not pulling your weight" is widely called out in terms of performance; *living by our values* is common currency in the modern workplace . . . We expect our colleagues to *have our backs* in the widest sense of that term, behaving in ways that respect our individuality but also recognizes our responsibility to the shared endeavor.

This is why leaders in business and public life have a particular responsibility to live by the values they espouse. In the UK, a number of senior politicians and key advisors have been exposed in flouting the social distancing and lockdown directives—survey after survey has shown that their behavior lost the trust of the British public at a critical time in controlling the pandemic. The reason is simple—those who make the rules must measure up to them more stringently than most—for not to do so is *freeriding* in its worst possible form.

Leaders must also recognize that their behavior is a model

for others and with this comes responsibility that can sometimes transcend our interest and beliefs. In the US, President Trump's long-time refusal to wear masks and faux-macho posturing in the face of the virus will undoubtedly have cost many lives. Imagine the doubt that would have been sown if the same bravado were applied to the efficacy of a vaccine? As I write this article, Israel is leading the world in the inoculation of its citizens—interestingly, Prime Minister Netanyahu was very publicly one of the first in line.

Looking to the immediate future, I expect the scientific evidence will win out: that our desire to end the misery of lockdown—not to mention the avoidable loss of life—will create sufficient incentive without compulsion. Many of those who are disinclined to take the vaccine will reassess their views as the benefits become clear; the peddlers of conspiracies will no doubt find other outlets to feed their toxic paranoia. Ultimately, good sense will prevail.

And on this note, I'm hopeful in a wider sense. For Margaret Keenan was right—the vaccine is indeed the best early birthday present—not just for her, but for the world. And, as those rays of light I spoke of earlier begin to brighten, there is surely an opportunity to show what collective will and community endeavor can achieve. We are bigger—and better—than the *freeriders* in our midst. We can (and should) legislate and compel where absolutely necessary, but our most powerful weapon is to actively play our part, living by the values and behaviors we would hope others do too, and quietly dishonoring those who do not.

AFTERWORDS

. . . we are dwarfs astride the shoulders of giants. We master their wisdom and move beyond it. Due to their wisdom, we grow wise and are able to say all that we say, but not because we are greater than they.

Isaiah di Trani

THE COINS IN OUR POCKETS

THE COINS WE CARRY in our pockets are in many ways remarkable. Their heritage, as tokens of nominal value, stretches back to the very origins of trade. From the first crudely minted discs to today's complex designs, coins have enabled more than mere exchange: they facilitate our movement, support complex transactions, and are founded on communal trust. In a sense, they are a physical embodiment of millennia of human industry and invention—the ultimate everyday symbol of our collective achievements.

And yet, how often do we stop to examine them? Unless you're a numismatist like me, I suspect you seldom give them much thought. Which is a pity, for their designs alone can remind us of what we owe to others and the past. On every US coin, for example, is minted the motto, *e pluribus unum* (Out of Many, One) which refers to the union of states and the idea that we are more than the sum of our parts.

In writing the essays in this book, I've come to reflect on my personal journey, not only as a leader in business, but more broadly as a father, statistician, sports fan. No matter how we define ourselves or measure our success, I'm more conscious than ever that unless we live like Robinson Crusoe, we must all give thanks and pay tribute to others. Those of us who've risen to senior positions have an even greater obligation to do so.

Malcom Gladwell, in his debut book, *The Tipping Point*, wrote of the importance of Mavens—those persons whose knowledge and wisdom plays a vital role in the adoption of popular trends. Often, in organizations and social movements, we can trace seminal decisions back to their influence. At a personal level too, most of us can name individuals to whom—either directly or by way of connected thread— we can link the progress and direction of our lives.

Early in my career, I was fortunate enough to work at a financial organization for a leader who combined the expectations of hard work and analysis with a softer side that took time to encourage a young man to make the most of his talents. It was through him that I first learned the value of communicating with care and the power of modesty as a means to motivate. He showed me too—and with great patience on his part—that mistakes are part of our progress.

Later, on my first appointment as a CEO, I was blessed with a chairman who taught me much about the need for firmness of mind. Leadership—and indeed many of the big decisions in our lives—can be beset by doubtful voices, which, if we allow them to become too loud, result only in mixed messages and vacillation. It was through him that I learned to marry an openness to new ideas with a necessary clarity of purpose and direction. As we've seen, Bertrand Russell, in *The Conquest of Happiness*, talked of something similar: when faced with conflicting options, he said, we must act on the best available information, and then hold to our decision, unless or until there is clear evidence to the contrary.

The reference to Russell illustrates that great minds have never been more available to us. Bookshops and libraries are a wellspring of wisdom—so too the internet, if we use it with care. In this respect, some of my mentors are people I've never met—and yet through their works, I'm constantly learning, continually challenged, forever curious. It has long struck me as a sadness that so many college graduates give up their studies on beginning their careers. That's not to say we should all be academics in our spare time, but maintaining that essential curiosity feeds and pays tribute to the wonderful gift that is our collective understanding.

I learned this from my father, a quintessential polymath and my greatest mentor and friend in life; the debt I owe to him and his gentle influence cannot be overstated. Of course, when I say *debt*, I really mean gratitude for, like all the best mentors, he would not wish for payment. This reminds me of a former colleague who had an unrelenting belief in our duty to make better decisions, seeking always to test and improve for the benefit of all. He was one of the most intelligent people I've ever met and yet, far from displaying the hubris of certainty, he tenaciously challenged the status quo, blending a scientific mindset with a kindness and warmth that spoke to—and quietly enhanced—my personal values.

And isn't this what great mentors do?

Very few of us experience a "Road to Damascus" moment that changes our outlook overnight. Indeed, my core beliefs in liberalism, meritocracy, and a duty of care to those less fortunate, have not radically changed since my college days. But by learning from the perspectives and wisdom of others around me, those convictions have been enriched and refined. I hope this never ceases; I hope too—as they would remind me—that I remain open to evangelism of a sort, for there is merit in radical thinking if we are to make step changes. *Liberté, égalité, fraternité*—the motto of the French Revolution (and on the reverse of its Euro coins)—is a useful reminder that the very values we hold most dear were once heretical thoughts.

But whether our knowledge is founded on education or epiphany makes little difference to our dues. Science and mathematics are a ten-thousand-year endeavor; democracy—and much of our philosophy—comes from ancient Greece; the very languages we use to communicate are founded on social constructs. Similarly, today, our industries, our health services, our transportation . . . and the careers and opportunities which come with them, are built on the efforts of our forebears and contemporaries.

In writing these essays, I'm clearer than ever that the idea of the self-made person is contradictory to an interdependent, multicultural, increasingly global world. We are, all of us, carried on the shoulders of giants. Even a genius like Leonardo da Vinci served as an apprentice; those of us less gifted are—in a sense—bound to a lifetime of learning from others. We should see that as joy—*not a trial*; as a credit; *not a debit*—in the balance sheet of life. Or perhaps, as two sides of the same coin—the many and the one, each dependent on the other.

TURNING THE TIDE

SHORTLY AFTER TAKING OFFICE, President Joe Biden gave a speech on the progress of the Covid-19 vaccination program. He offered hope for a July 4th Independence Day and asked that all Americans work together, playing their part to help reinstate the personal freedoms that we previously took for granted. In a refreshingly candid response to those who would lift restrictions immediately, he summarised the prerequisite with one word—time.

President Biden was addressing a particular and immediate issue, and his approach was more driven by scientific advice than any deeper reflection. His reasoning was simply that to secure the progress already made, we needed time for more people to be vaccinated, time to assess the impact on transmission, time for the tide to irreversibly turn.

But listening to the speech, I was struck not so much by his welcome appeals to common cause and collective endeavor, but by the contrast between his plea for patience and the expectations of progress that we have come to expect. Indeed, he himself had set ambitious goals for his first "hundred days" in office, a phrase that's commonplace in the world of business, fueled by the belief that pace is vital to success.

There is much truth in this view. While the hundred days slogan can be an overused catchphrase, its underlying principle is that progress requires affirmative action; that indecision at moments of change leads only to entrenchment and resistance. Or in plainer Anglo Saxon, sleepy organizations sometimes need a kick up the proverbial . . . !

Few businesses making an acquisition or merger today, would be encouraged by their advisors to reflect on the intricacies of every adjustment they propose to make. The mainstream view is that if the consequence of pace is occasionally some collateral damage results, then this needs to be seen in the context of the counterfactual stasis that comes with prevarication.

We believe, too, that change is coming ever faster. As long ago as the 1960s, Gordon Moore predicted that the power of integrated circuit boards would double every couple of years, leading to exponential digital progress. Only now is Moore's Law reaching its threshold with compound (not absolute) rates, beginning to slow. The advance in technology is unquestionably the most transformative change of the last half century, it's reach touching every aspect of our lives, from medicine to machinery, warfare to welfare, education to employment.

But I wonder if we are not sometimes too dazzled by the consultants, the statistics, and an over-emphasis on digital technology as the benchmark of change.

In writing *Fair Value*, I have reflected deeply on the beliefs which have underpinned my life and career. And the most striking thing is not how much they have altered but rather how little they have—and how gradual and considered their evolution has been. We do not transform our beliefs overnight, and nor can our behaviors (individual or collective) adapt in the way of digital components. The same is true of our societies and the communities and organizations which are their constituent parts.

The reality is that more profound change takes time.

The values and instincts which guide our paths are deeply embedded. Our sense of community, the people we love, our faiths and aspirations. All these do not alter at speed. This is why dictatorships have consistently failed to suppress a desire for freedom—or for that matter, why new democracies often face resistance from within. In business, the idea that we can culturally transform organizations in short order is usually a recipe for disappointment if not outright failure.

None of this is to suggest we should not address injustices with the urgency they deserve. The slow progress on issues such as gender equality, diversity and inclusion, educational opportunity and true meritocracy are a stain on our democracies. It is right that we demand progress and call out those organizations which make only token efforts, just as we should look at ourselves and be honest in declaring the ways we might do more.

The environmental crisis is a case in point; there is a clear responsibility to make bold changes today, even if the impacts will not be felt for decades to come—indeed, that's exactly why we need to act now. But even then, we need also to be patient, and mindful that parts of the world are less well placed to take the radical steps we might wish to see, and less well informed of the consequences of delay.

Meanwhile, we are all impatient for those changes that are dear to our hearts. Like those who would ease the pandemic restrictions tomorrow, I too have concerns that I wish were addressed more swiftly. In the US and the Europe there are whole regions that have been left behind by the impacts of globalization. Their people want action, a reversal of the trend, a recognition that what's been lost needs replacing with more than just hope.

I have my doubts on the swift achievability of that goal, for experience has shown it to be an intractable problem. As with so many of the challenges we face, the ways forward are myriad and often untravelled, and in common with the opening theme of this piece, they will take time.

In writing these essays I've come increasingly to understand that in pursuing change for the good, we must first and foremost set our compass to the values that offer the best opportunities for hope and flourishing. For only this way can we navigate the paths that will inevitably lead us in less than straight lines. We need also to recognize that time is part of the equation of progress, and that a little patience can help us resolve it more neatly and completely than our restless natures might wish.

The tide as they say will turn only on its hour.

CPSIA information can be obtained
at www.ICGtesting.com
Printed in the USA
LVHW111136010921
696661LV00003B/326

9 781646 634576